ROUTLEDGE LIBRARY EDITIONS: SOCRATES

Volume 1

SOCRATES AMONG HIS PEERS

SOCRATES AMONG HIS PEERS
Three Dialogues

OWEN GRAZEBROOK

LONDON AND NEW YORK

First published in 1927 by Kegan Paul, Trench, Trubner & Co., Ltd.

This edition first published in 2019
by Routledge
2 Park Square, Milton Park, Abingdon, Oxon OX14 4RN

and by Routledge
711 Third Avenue, New York, NY 10017

Routledge is an imprint of the Taylor & Francis Group, an informa business

All rights reserved. No part of this book may be reprinted or reproduced or utilised in any form or by any electronic, mechanical, or other means, now known or hereafter invented, including photocopying and recording, or in any information storage or retrieval system, without permission in writing from the publishers.

Trademark notice: Product or corporate names may be trademarks or registered trademarks, and are used only for identification and explanation without intent to infringe.

British Library Cataloguing in Publication Data
A catalogue record for this book is available from the British Library

ISBN: 978-1-138-61842-8 (Set)
ISBN: 978-0-429-45011-2 (Set) (ebk)
ISBN: 978-1-138-62396-5 (Volume 1) (hbk)
ISBN: 978-1-138-62398-9 (Volume 1) (pbk)
ISBN: 978-0-429-46105-7 (Volume 1) (ebk)

Publisher's Note
The publisher has gone to great lengths to ensure the quality of this reprint but points out that some imperfections in the original copies may be apparent.

Disclaimer
The publisher has made every effort to trace copyright holders and would welcome correspondence from those they have been unable to trace.

SOCRATES
AMONG HIS PEERS

Three Dialogues

BY
OWEN GRAZEBROOK

LONDON
KEGAN PAUL, TRENCH, TRUBNER & Co., Ltd.
Broadway House : 68-74 Carter Lane, E.C.
1927

PRINTED IN GREAT BRITAIN BY HEADLEY BROTHERS,
18, DEVONSHIRE STREET, E.C.2 ; AND ASHFORD, KENT

CONTENTS

	PAGE
NIGHT AND THE DREAM — — — —	I
THE VERDICT — — — — —	63
THE CITY OF GOD — — — —	125

PREFACE

In the 2,300 years that have passed since Socrates died we have learnt much of mechanics and still more of mechanism, but it is doubtful if we comprehend any better either the Universe or the Universal, or if the theses of Darwin, or the advent of Neo-Lamarckians have made us any kinder to the animals or to the unfortunate ; nor, as yet, have the formulæ of Einstein illuminated for us that Space which Newton circumscribed and Plato comprehended.

We have lost quite definitely that restraint or sense of proportion which the Greek civilisation produced in their artists, and we have learnt to associate goodness with dulness, and to credit the sinner with the wit that is more often found with saints : the Greeks did not suffer from these illusions.

Although the typewriter and penny post are not entirely responsible for the disappearance of good letter-writing, or the loud speaker for the deterioration of good conservation, the decay of both arts began with the Industrial Revolution, which has shortened our leisure and dulled our delight.

PREFACE

Mr Greville, the diarist, leisured but not wholly delightful, writing in December, 1851, laments the death of one of his circle, famous in his day for his conversation. " There are, however, so many more good writers than good talkers, and the two qualities are so rarely united in the same person, that we owe a debt of gratitude to LUTTRELL for having cultivated his conversational powers rather than his literary powers, and for having adorned and delighted society for so many years with his remarkable vivacity and wit."

Other writers, more ambitious than Mr Greville, have essayed to reproduce the wit and the charm of the great talkers of the past ; but it would seem that print cannot convey a charm which must depend on the voice and the manner of the speaker quite as much as the matters on which he speaks, and it is as impossible to recreate the illusion by recording the scattered conceits of Sydney Smith, or the asides of Disraeli, as to make a necklace of quality from the ill-assorted and dusty gems in the window of an old curiosity shop.

The Greeks of the age of Pericles had both the leisure and the civilisation to bring the art of conversation to a high pitch ; and through the pages of Plato we can picture the polished urbane and courteous host plying that art which needs the analogies of fencing to explain or elucidate its refinements.

PREFACE

In the conversations recorded, the fables, beautiful in themselves, have a direct bearing on what is being discussed, in contradistinction to those stories with the inevitable Scotch, Irish, or American patois, which lacerate the oratory of one Continent, and the dinner-tables of our own land.

Those conversations, we may imagine, owed something to the clearness of the Athenian climate and sky, as neither the speakers nor the audience seemed to be hampered by those restraints of prudery or false piety which the English climate or the taint of Puritanism imposes on our table-talk.

On the other hand, it is by no means certain that we should appreciate to-day the presence of Socrates at our supper-parties. He would drink, I suspect, a great deal of port—without which conversation is sometimes thin—and some might be tempted to say with St Joan : How long, O Lord, how long ?

In the three dialogues that compose my book I have tried to describe what an Athenian company might have said had they, too, been discussing Death and the Hereafter ; Justice ; and the Kingdom of Heaven. I imagine that very much the same things would be said to-day. Our Immortality is independent of a Prayer Book, however Revised ; our civil authorities are still

PREFACE

puzzled to know how to deal with the Persistent Just Man; and the Kingdom of Heaven is still unstormed.

These dialogues imply no technical knowledge of philosophy. Jowett himself recommends, in his preface, even business-men to write on these or kindred matters.

In conclusion, I must thank Mr Bridges and Mr Drinkwater for their courtesy in allowing me to quote from their works; and Messrs Longmans for the quotation from *The Spirit of Man*.

OWEN F. GRAZEBROOK.

Himley, March, 1927.

NIGHT AND THE DREAM

NIGHT AND THE DREAM

O ask ye no more of me. Were I to tell you
    more words of his,
Ye would burst your bonds, no roof nor door could
    restrain you.—*Jellaludin*.

    Nor, when our days are done,
    And the last utterance of doom must fall
    Is the doom anything
    Memorable for its apparelling,
    The bearing of man facing it is all.

        Abraham Lincoln, by JOHN DRINKWATER.

CHARACTERS

Triptolemus – – – The Narrator

Agathon – – – The Playwright

Eurymachus – – An Ordinary Citizen

Critias – – – The Politician

Xenophon – – – The Author

Plato – – –

Aristophanes – – The Comedy Writer

Socrates – – –

The memory of Socrates was kept fresh in the mind of his times by the lectures and teaching of Plato, but after his death any of those who had anything personal to impart of the Martyr were listened to with eagerness.

The scene of this Dialogue is laid in Athens, and from his couch Triptolemus, who is now an old man, is telling a group of young men what he can remember of his last conversation with Socrates and the other companions of his Master.

NIGHT AND THE DREAM

I CAN remember quite well the last time I was with Socrates, and if it would interest you, I will tell you as far as I can what happened.

Two years before he was put to death, I left Athens to go to Megara, and did not return until I learnt that the City was once more safe for democracy, so that it is impossible for me to tell you of my own knowledge what happened when my friend died, or in what way he met death face to face. But if you are sufficiently patient with me I will tell you what was said that night, that I remember so well; and you will understand how the business of death should be approached, for it was on this subject that Socrates spoke.

I shall never forget what Socrates said that night, but I must warn you first, if you would rightly follow the importance of his teaching, that many things were said before he spoke, which it is necessary that you should hear. The occasion was a supper party at the House of Agathon. Many others of my friends were present, men who were well known to your fathers, so that their names should not be unfamiliar to you : Agathon, then a very old man, and soon to die, and Xenophon

NIGHT AND THE DREAM

and Aristophanes. Plato's name you should all know, he was always with Socrates, and the one, I think, who understood him best, and in my opinion the best suited to record the words of our Master.

It was in the early summer, for to each of us had been given a chaplet of young grapes which the gardener had thinned out that day from his vines, and it comes back to me that Aristophanes refused at first to put on what he said was an indelicate, womanly, and impious garment, and we had some difficulty to persuade Xenophon that Aristophanes did not always mean what he said.

After we had eaten we talked far into the night as was our wont, and, among other things, discussed especially how hard it was to live well, and we had finally agreed that only by becoming wise and old at the same time, was it possible— when Agathon, I think, said that that was not the same thing as living well. Perhaps we had not been thinking or talking very exactly since Socrates would not join us in drinking or conversation, for he had left his couch between Plato and Aristophanes to go out and sit in the porch by himself—this, as perhaps I have told you before, was often his custom. At any rate, after we had all spoken on one side or the other, as sometimes happens, a sudden silence overtook us.

NIGHT AND THE DREAM

Eurymachus it was who broke the silence—Eurymachus, who generally listened rather than led the conversation, saying, almost to himself: " Tho' it were hard to live well—it is harder still to die."

Such a remark coming from one who had never experienced the lust of battle, or even learnt to endure unnecessary hardships with the patience that is the hall-mark, one might say, of a soldier, made Critias laugh—but before he could say anything Eurymachus continued: " I know quite well why you laugh, for you, Critias, have already faced death many times, and each time, I am sure, with a laugh and a jest, but it is one thing to meet death as a competitor at the games as it were striving for the prizes of victory (which is what a soldier must do), and quite another to invite him into your house as a bed-fellow. It seems to me, after listening to all that has been said about living aright, or at least doing such things as are agreeable to the Gods and yet not too unpleasant for our neighbours—that it is a far more difficult thing to die well. For even if we obtain that ripe old age which you say can best teach us how to order our days, there is another side to old age, as the poet says :

There is no trouble worse than length of life,
Old age hath all the ills that flesh is heir to—
Vain thoughts and powerless deeds, and vanish't mind.

7

NIGHT AND THE DREAM

"So that some of us may come to the end without having amassed sufficient wisdom to know how to die. In any case when it comes to dying, we can place no reliance on those rules which we may have agreed upon as being suitable for teaching us how to live, since Death has no lot nor parcel with life, and what may have been of good service in our dealings with our neighbours or the Gods cannot avail us in dealing with Death who will take everything from us, and tho' you will tell me—and I will agree with you—that certain rules of conduct have proved generally helpful in the business of living—none of you can give me any practical experience of dying."

Before either Critias or Aristophanes could speak, Agathon replied—for he saw how deeply the thought of these things had exercised Eurymachus, and feared lest these others might say something that would hurt :

" All that you say is true—but on this subject I can speak with more authority than any of you in so far as it is most likely that Death is nearest to me, and as Eurymachus has suggested he has become increasingly about my board and about my bed.

"As to living well—my course is so nearly run, I must leave it to you who one day soon will gather around my funeral pyre, to decide how much wisdom I have been able to collect as I became

NIGHT AND THE DREAM

an old man, or if, on the other hand, old age has found me vain and powerless, as some of the poets would seem to suggest is a possibility. Let us consider this problem of facing Death. When I was a young man I feared to die—and rightly I think—since Nature not having finished her dealings with my body she feared perhaps lest her purpose might be in vain—but now, when I am in the natural course of things soon to be excused from the duties and toils laid upon me at my birth—the distaste—if I use no harsher word for his presence—grows less. Not that I no longer fear—for no mortal man can be wholly unafraid of Death, but many things having become burdensome, such, I can relinquish almost gladly —in some such way Nature modifies the fears of old age after she has diminished the joys of life and softened the bitterness of grief."

Before any of the others could speak Plato broke in : " You talk as if this, our friend, Death, was not merely an end in himself but an end for each one of us as well. I cannot believe this any more than I can believe that ' Vain thought or Vanish't mind ' can ever be your lot Agathon. Do you not believe that we shall all of us meet again after death and be able to discuss our experience rather than our fear of this dying ? Not here, or in our mortal bodies, but yonder, and in some other guise."

NIGHT AND THE DREAM

But then we were all ready to speak, for on such a subject all of us had at some time or other formed an opinion, and thoughts of Death and the life that may be hereafter were specially suited to the time and place, for we had finished eating and the wine was passing round, and the stars could be seen peeping out over the City beyond the head of Socrates as he sat in the porch.

Critias, however, drowned us all—ás was fitting in a public man—" If I was not certain that I was speaking to an educated audience I should keep silence " (Aristophanes whispered, but quite loud—" as if he could "), " but when Plato trades upon my good humour and love of peace, in defiance of my finer feelings, I must speak. When I die—if there is anything of me left after my struggles—must I sit silent and listen for ever to Immortals in debate ? Can one who shared the burdens of Pericles accept the rhetoric of Olympus without a protest ? Since I cannot write the sort of plays that you write Agathon—plays that will each night please the whole company of Heaven— and even you may become weary of being crowned every night—must I for ever make speeches in answer to Apollo—that is if Plato's threat is indeed true. And what will our friend here do in Olympus ? " and he pointed to Aristophanes so that I wondered if he had heard the whispering. " Most of his plays are far too dangerous to bear

NIGHT AND THE DREAM

repetition in the City, much less are they suitable among the Clouds, shall I say, and before such a touchy audience—if you will allow the word—men of Athens. Why, he would present Hebe as a fish-wife and Love as a hetaira, and I cannot think the Thunderer would sit as complacently as Cleon—if indeed the Thunderer still retains his position. Let me quote you the words of the Son of Peleus :

> You may make oxen and sheep your prey,
> Gather together tripods and the tawny manes of horses,
> But none can make the soul of man return by theft or
> craft when once it has escaped.

"No, my friends, Death is inevitable and the end of all things, of our life here, and our bodies, our suppers and our discussions, our friends and our foes.

"We gain nothing by fearing Death, as we rightly fear necessity or deformity." We must accept it as we accept a vote in the Assembly. Critias always spoke in private as if he was addressing the Assembly, and used to wave his arms about like a madman, or an actor which disconcerted those who were not used to him. Here Xenophon, contrary to his custom, volunteered an opinion on an abstract subject :

"Your words are almost that of the poet :

> Alone of Gods, Death loves not gifts—with him
> No sacrifice no incense aught avail.
> He hath no altar and no hymns of gladness,
> Prayer stands aloof from him—Persuasion fails.

NIGHT AND THE DREAM

"So that if we cannot propitiate this Death, as it would seem, nor fight him, for it is of no avail, we must needs subdue ourselves unto him. But for myself, I cannot believe that Death is indeed the absolute end of each one of us. I must admit that I can give no reason for my belief, nevertheless, it has always been with me. Perhaps it is an instinct, like that of a pigeon who is always able to find her way home from whatever direction or however far away she is started on a flight."

As he finished speaking he turned to Plato as if to help him—for Xenophon never had the gift of explaining his thoughts—Aristophanes said once that he had no thoughts to explain—but all the same there is a sturdy commonsense about Xenophon that grows on you as you get to know him better, and compels you to listen to what he says. In some way or other he attracted young men especially, and if ever you meet him you will find it out for yourselves. But Plato refused to speak : " for if I did," he said, " Aristophanes would die—an object lesson to us all perhaps—but not even his example in dying before our eyes, discreetly or otherwise, could reconcile me to his loss to-night." He turned round to him and said, " Come now and deliver yourself of what is churning inside you, or in your own words say :

I am the dog. I bark aloud for you.

NIGHT AND THE DREAM

Do you remember that trick of Aristophanes—when he was pleased he would push his wreath more to one side or the other—sometimes pulling it down with his left hand, or dragging it forward with his right, until it settled almost over the end of his nose—and when Plato had finished speaking we could all see how pleased he was that words from his own plays should be quoted as it were a chorus before he came on the stage, for his wreath had settled itself well over his right eye.

" What is the good of my saying anything," he began, grumbling, " when I have finished—and I warn you all before I begin that I shall not sheathe the sword, as Critias would say, until I have delivered myself of everything that occurs to me—when I have finished, silence and darkness will be round about me ; and Xenophon will be wondering audibly if I am serious, while Agathon, conscious, as always, of his rich rectitude, his reputation, the ripeness of his old age and his even more than distinguished grey hairs will make excuses for me."

And Aristophanes almost hissed out the words for he disliked Agathon. He then continued :

" Eurymachus will take it all for gospel—Critias will listen only that he may treasure up some trifle in the nature of an epigram that he can palm off as his own—and still be jealous. Plato will laugh at me—and that fellow (and he pointed

NIGHT AND THE DREAM

out towards the night) will not even listen. I believe he is frightened lest I bring him on the stage again." But even tho' he spoke these last words so loud that Socrates must needs hear him, he did not come back or reply, so Aristophanes continued :

"The only true words I have heard to-night, so far, are that we cannot avoid dying ; for that reason I never think of Death if I can help it— it is enough for me to see the City and all its well being sickening from all these new-fangled virtues—nothing brings on death quicker than a surfeit of good things. If you would refrain from making speeches in the flesh, Critias, the virtue of the City and the Assembly would not be tried so high, and you would feel fresher when the time comes to argue with the Immortals— whose virtue, by the way, they say is fireproof. But to return, I can give Eurymachus the one and only rule for a satisfactory death, and that is to get it over as quickly as possible. To linger for long over the final—may I say, act, is to be like a hen (after the rhetorician possibly the most stupid of animals) which, even after its neck is wrung, persists in flapping its wings and pretending to be alive.

"My advice to you all is this—when once you have made up your mind, or had it made up for you that Death can no longer be avoided—

NIGHT AND THE DREAM

believe me the effect is much the same—Die—at once.

"Should you seek confirmation from the poet, I can quote as well as you :

Bury me soon that I may pass the gates of Hades."

Aristophanes paused for a moment to drink, and, looking round the table, said : " A second appeal to the same poet seems more applicable to some of you, and should comfort you :

After the event even the fool is wise.

But none of you will pay any serious attention to what I say, for because my plays are really witty, you think they lack morals, and because I am serious, you say I am trying to be funny, and yet it is because of my gifts that I am a prophet. The Gifts of Comedy and Prophecy are the same.

"This is my trouble ", he went on ; " and no one who ventures out as a writer of Comedy can expect anything else. Had I the gift "—and here he looked pointedly at Agathon—" which some of you enjoy, of saying stupid things with an air of piety, or had I the gift which Plato possesses of wrapping up his wisdom in a honeycomb, you would attend to what I say, and even go home and write down my words that you could refresh your memories when the occasion demanded it—or had I the mien and appearance of Cassandra,

NIGHT AND THE DREAM

or her natural gift for spontaneous rhapsody—
you would record my words even if only to confound your children with these prophecies as
your own—when they had become accomplished
facts, as they assuredly will. But since I show
you yourselves and your ideals without distor-
tion and false emphasis, and as they actually
are, rather than what you hope they are, you will
not try to believe me and take refuge in laughter.

" You say : ' Aristophanes is such an amusing
fellow ', ' he talks such good nonsense ', but I tell
you soon after you are dead, or long after you are
forgotten, your children will say : ' what mar-
vellous foresight Aristophanes displayed', 'how
well he foretold the future.'

"Comedy, my friends, can contain truth as well
as Tragedy, and is as well, if not better suited,
to enshrine (as a temple enshrines the statue and
the virtue of the Goddess) the laws of holy living—
and holy dying. All that is by the way—you
need not try to remember any of it Xenophon—
it will only confuse you. Listen to this :

" I have told you the Golden Rule for dying—
now for Death itself. You are all of you obsessed
with the importance of your own deaths. You
talk of Death almost as if he were himself an
Immortal, and as if he came as a special Messenger
from the Gods to each of us in our turn and at
the appropriate moment in the play.

NIGHT AND THE DREAM

"If I could keep talking long enough, I might convince you that our lives or our deaths so far from being a matter of concern to the Gods, leave them unmoved and unrepentent. We are no more important than any other of the dwellers under Heaven, and the airs we give ourselves are not justified.

"We cannot swim in water as well as the fishes or fly in the air as well as the birds, not in our own element can we run as swiftly as horses, or even sing as sweetly as the nightingale. At the best we can build houses more durable than the bee, but the earthquake will destroy both of them alike—and even the bee has advantages over us, because it can leave its sting behind. Indeed I think the animals are our superiors for they, at any rate, are content with what their parents have taught them, and are not for ever reaching out for experiments in their habits, or their governance. We are all merely the creatures of nature, and have no right to grumble when after having given us life, she takes it away and wantonly throws us away. For we can see how careless is this Mother of ours, when we observe her acting in exactly the same way with those of her children who have been born as plants or fruit bearing trees.

"Do not deceive yourselves in this matter by thinking that we are in any way wiser than

NIGHT AND THE DREAM

the animals around us. I am certain that your horse, for example, Xenophon, so far from thinking of you as his superior—and a God—is exercised rather by an imagination, which has created for him and his kind an equine Olympus where horse-like heroes spend eternity in neighing and eating and drinking and all such other delights as we depict for our own bodies when they have been used up in this world.

" No, my friends. I can listen to you more or less quietly, while you lay down rules for your conduct, and even mine, so long as we are both alive—being well aware how few of us obey these rules—but when you begin to talk of Death and try and convince yourselves—for you will not convince me—first that it is an evil, and secondly an end, and then go on to try to persuade yourselves that it is neither the one nor the other— why then I lose patience with you."

When Aristophanes had finished saying these things, Agathon turned to Plato to answer and take up the cudgels for us all, rather than provoke the wasp by saying anything himself, for he knew well enough how the land lay, as sailors say, and, of a truth we none of us would listen in patience to anyone else who said such hurtful things. Your fathers remember that, I expect.

" You are inspired to-night as usual Aristophanes," said Plato ; " so much so that I was

NIGHT AND THE DREAM

hoping you would continue until the morning that I might quote your own words against you.

> And shall not the High
> And infinite sky
> Go thundering on without end.

" But if you will not continue your thunder, I will do my best. Of the wisdom of the animal kingdom I dare not speak lest the company should rise together and confound me in equally inspired verse with the wise sayings of—shall I say the Hoopœ—and other delightful monsters of the same kind.

" This much I will admit, that all those who have the gift to see below the surface of things, and to peer into the future, are like owls who can see in the dark, and in general this City has always admired and has held in high honour persons having such gifts, even the Goddess herself has not thought it unworthy to take an owl unto herself. These gifts, too, we know are especially the portion of those who write our Comedies, but it seems on the other hand that such gifted persons are of all men most miserable. In return for this clearness of vision, those who are responsible for the disposal of these gifts either at birth or any other time, have taken away from the writers of Comedy all that sympathy with the struggles of the spirit, the love of simple things, and the generous hopes that,

NIGHT AND THE DREAM

for the rest of us, lighten the loads of our life and death.

"The writers of Tragedy have in some sort retained this simplicity, while those of us who are not so gifted retain these things in some form or other, and the one that I hold most precious is the Hope of Immortality.

"However much we may intend to lead a life that is acceptable to the Gods there will be times when we question—not indeed if the living of such a life is worth while as we say, for that is a conviction in our innermost being—at least it is with me—but whether the rule we have taken as our guide is comprehensive enough to cover and include the death that awaits us. Something akin to this I think, caused Eurymachus to say what he did about dying well, which incidentally enabled us to listen to the many and good things that have been said.

"As to whether Death is an end or not, it is hardly worth while arguing about it, if, by an end, we mean the finish of our life as we know it now, because it is obvious—even to me—that when I die, after a few days at most, you can none of you know me any more as I was. But, on the other hand, I too share that belief of Xenophon's—which was, he said, an instinct with him—that Death was not the end of everything, when we are touched on the shoulder and bidden away.

NIGHT AND THE DREAM

" I have often tried to find some reason that would support me in this belief that I might rely on something more stalwart than instinct."

" But does that matter ", said Agathon ; " I too have relied on this same blind feeling— but as I have grown older—it has become stronger rather than weaker, and so far as such things can become matters of reason and argument, I can find both in a knowledge in the Justice of the Gods."

This brought back Aristophanes, almost with a snarl. I think perhaps he disliked Agathon so much because he thought him effeminate, nor could he bring himself to like his plays, which in their day had been as successful as his own, though in a different way.

" I feel unwell ", he said, " and if any of you continue to talk in such a strain, I warn you all I shall be dangerously ill. You, Agathon, as far as appearances go—and we have little else to rely on—you are a good man. Anything I might say of your plays you will put down to prejudice —so I will only say that in spite of much evidence to the contrary—you are looked upon as a sensible and devout person. But when you fasten your intentions of continuing to exist as Agathon, first, on the Gods themselves, without even receiving their consent, by the way, and secondly, in their sense of justice—are you not almost—shall we

NIGHT AND THE DREAM

say—over-rating your personal importance and charm and so forth, and imputing fresh doubts on their justice—'if any', as the lawyers are accustomed to say.

"You have quoted the Son of Peleus"—but Agathon shook his head, and Plato said: "No, I was the guilty one." But Aristophanes for once was vehement and serious and scarcely stopped in his stride to continue: "If that is all you can hope for—the help of Olympus, the Justice of Olympus, your case is weak indeed.

"Let me quote you the words of Achilles when bereft of hope, and with distraction and agony, his boon companions, plucking aside the door of his tent to enter in, what was his cry, his last cry of despair? 'My Mother. The Olympian hath done all these things.'

"If you buoy yourself up with idle hopes, based on the kindness or the justice or even the existence of the Gods, miserable as you say that I and my kin must be, our plight is happier than yours for we have the courage to see what things shall be, and yet have no fear."

Plato answered him thus: "But if there be Gods, Aristophanes (and that same sort of Immortal Powers, though each one of us may call them by different names, must rule, there can be no doubt), we can be certain that they will know Justice, though it may well be that

NIGHT AND THE DREAM

the justice that is Everlasting may not be justice as we can conceive it, since Justice, belonging to the Eternal things is of necessity God-like and Immortal. Justice is also a necessity to man, in some form or other—and to me it seems reasonable, to put it no higher than that, to believe that having been pitchforked into this world without conscious act of our own, some reward, or it may be punishment, in accordance with their deserts, must be given to those who have been compelled to pass their existence in this world. Otherwise it would not seem, according to our ideas at any rate, fair that those who have struggled so hard, yourself for example, to accomplish what you would fain do, while others—it may be—less handicapped with good things, have been content to do nothing.

" But to go back to where I was before Agathon helped me out with that speech which caused you to say what you did—we have all been talking of Immortality and Death as if they were connected the one with the other, but for my part they seem akin only so long as we think that the one is a sequence of the other, and even that I do not believe.

" I will try and explain what I mean by an example—you, Agathon, and you Aristophanes, must both die, yet I cannot think that by becoming dead you will become alike. On the other

NIGHT AND THE DREAM

hand should you both continue your existence yonder, it is not too difficult to imagine that in many respects you will continue akin to your former and existing selves each to each—Agathon perhaps ruling in another Phæacia, Antinouslike, gracious and moderate in all things and yet still Agathon.

" While as for you"—turning to Aristophanes who was still a little flushed and possibly angry with himself for ceasing to be always cool and ironical—"this epitaph, was written indeed for another, but will apply to the things you will enjoy doing, wherever you are, and unless you are careful I will carve these words on your tomb", and slowly he recited the inscription that Alcæus had written for the tomb of the satirist.

> Hipponax is buried here.   Nought the ground will bear,
> Save the deadly nightshade or the sour wild pear.
> Tricking thirsty travellers—just the sort of jest
> Hipponax would revel in—were he not At Rest.

"But let us just for a moment consider that some of you were right and that Death is indeed merely a Messenger sent to each of us in turn, at the appropriate moment to call us on to another stage. We must entertain such a one with the kindliest feelings that we can, remembering always that he comes as a guest, although not perhaps entirely at our own request, but as a herald is considered sacred even among the barbarians,

NIGHT AND THE DREAM

we as citizens of no mean City, dare not treat this Death too harshly when he comes.

" Most of us in our different ways are prepared for the likelihood (if I use no stronger expression) of existence on that other stage—and again with quite different opinions as to what that stage will be like—for myself I am as certain of the one as of the other, and my hope of some kind of Immortality is more often present with me than any apprehension of the arrival of the messenger to take me away—but this again I believe is yet another gift of Nature, our Mother, when we were born so that we can, if we will, partake of the next life before we have put away the garments of this present one.

" I will not quote the words of any poet, although they are full of such thoughts as these, expressed perhaps with more liberty than I am allowed—but this hope and steadfastness of purpose, with which I claim we are endowed in order to accomplish our Destiny afterwards, is immortalised for the Hellenes for ever in our greatest heritage—the Story of the Wanderer.

" You know how that Man of Many Devices kept steadfast through many trials and the enmity of the Host of Heaven. Was not his passionate desire for his home and his wife, that alone enabled him to triumph, something higher than the instinct of the pigeon flying home ? Was

NIGHT AND THE DREAM

it not also something greater than hope that sustained Penelope to endure unto the end? Nor has the poet denied us the end of the Odyssey and the home coming. Of such a nature is the hunger of the soul for its eternal abode. Never despairing even though flesh and blood as we say conspire together to prevent the fulfilment of her desire. This hunger and thirst after right dealing is, I think, born in the soul and is indeed part of our Immortality, so that nothing can destroy the Eternal principle that resides within us—the body may be marred or crippled, but nothing external can kill the soul."

With some such words as these Plato finished speaking, and I, who so far had not spoken, said such things as occurred to me—but whether good or bad at any rate it was my words which brought back Socrates, whose speech I shall shortly relate to you.

"All that may or may not be true", I said, "when I hear you speaking I can believe all that you say and take courage—yet I am often conscious of having to face that touch on the shoulder from Death the familiar—and I should like you to go on talking so that my fears of this also would be charmed away."

But Plato shook his head. "On such a night as this I cannot believe in Death—so that I am not able to comfort or arm you against perils that

NIGHT AND THE DREAM

seem so distant and far away. Yet when children are frightened of the dark, or thunder, and the slaves that are their guardians are not to be found because they too are afraid, some one has to come and drive away the terrors that assail them."

So speaking, he got up and went out into the porch where Socrates was still sitting away from the company—and touching him on the shoulder he said " Master, the night is far gone, and some of us are afraid of a spectre, Death. Treat me as a Herald who summons you to return with me, and drive away the perils of the night."

Socrates, spoke for the first time that night (after looking at Plato as if his mind having come back from the realms of thought had returned to earth, and first beheld what he loved most dearly).

" But how can I comfort you ? "

To which Plato replied :

" It is the duty of the Master at all times to drive away the foes of the household even though they be the fears of children."

And Socrates, rising from his seat in the porch, came into the light (for the oil was still burning in some of the lamps). As he came to his couch he picked up the wreath which still lay there, and having put it on with due solemnity he asked, " Is it necessary that I also should fear Death ?

NIGHT AND THE DREAM

" Certainly, Socrates ", he said, " if you intend to drive this shadow away from our company."

" Perhaps it would be as well, otherwise you might say that my shouting was not the genuine variety—whereas if I can become, like you, really terrified and could succeed in encouraging myself, I should be doing us both a good turn at the same time."

By this time Agathon had aroused the slaves, who had gone to sleep fearing nothing, neither Death, nor the anger of their Master, and these placed before us fresh wine. Socrates filled for himself a great flagon such as he alone could drink without distress, and said : " If at this moment I was face to face with Death, I could think of no better libation than this—' Nay, seek not to speak soothingly to me of Death, glorious Odysseus.' "

And then he drank.

When Socrates was talking at length, and I warn you that his speech was a long one, he would fix his eyes on the table before him until he had occasion to address one of the company in particular, or made a more astounding statement than usual, when he would look up, and opening his eyes very wide, make his assertion in his blandest voice. It was thus that he began, turning his head towards Agathon and saying :

28

NIGHT AND THE DREAM

"I must be very careful what I say, for frightened though I appear, it is as nothing to the dangers I risk talking of Death, for you will remember that I have often warned you that false words are not only evil in themselves, but they infect the soul with evil, both him who speaks and those who listen.

" It will be wiser therefore if I confine myself to telling you a tale that has some bearing on Death, and this Immortality of which you have been talking.

" It is not one of those stories which rhapsodists and other inspired persons, when like conquerors they gather rewards, have so often told of heroes, but rather of an ordinary man like ourselves.

" When I was in Egypt, it was my habit, and some of you know it well enough, to talk with anyone I came across either on the wharves, or in the market place, or indeed anywhere, who seemed prepared to talk, or to have anything out of the common to relate. This has always been my custom, and by such means I have been able to learn many things which conversations with the learned have for some reason or other been unable to supply.

" On this occasion, likewise, I learned much, for I can assure you that even sailors, when talking of what they know from experience or what they have done, are quite equal to teaching

NIGHT AND THE DREAM

the wisest of us—but this especially remains in my mind—this story that I propose to tell you, which was told me by a soldier, and that you may believe me better, I will tell you his name was Simonides.

" One night he was on guard inside a temple wherein lay the dead body of a man who had been killed in a fight between the slave-owners and their slaves in the quarries for which the district was famous, for when the overseers had conquered, and were rounding up the slaves with whips in their hands, they had found the body of this man, dead indeed as they thought. But on the third day, as his body lay before the altar, and with the due rites incomplete, he returned to life and related what had befallen him and what he had seen, and among the first to the man who had been on guard over his body, and this is what he told of that sojourn in the House of Death.

" He said that he had been surprised by two slaves who fell upon him before he could loosen his sword, and as he struggled with them he stumbled, and remembered nothing more until he became aware of a vast and empty space, and not finding his trusty and well-known body, which had been mislaid, and being lonely and frightened alike from the loss of his body, and the vastness of the place where he was, his spirit

NIGHT AND THE DREAM

wept bitterly seeking everywhere for what had been lost.

"Nor were these the only terrors that assailed him, for, being without sight or sound of anything living, or even another soul, a great numbness came over him, and his soul, if soul it was, seemed to be encompassed by a bitter cold wind, more cold and bitter than any wind could be on the earth, and he seemed to partake of this cold wind unto himself. This, he said, was the first terror of death, and he compared his plight with that of a tyrant, since such as these must carry the most grievous burdens, isolated and without companions, and that was his own condition, only far worse in that there was neither wife nor child nor friend to comfort him, neither was there any to console with him in his evil condition. And his sense of isolation was akin to nakedness, a shrinking in upon himself, for he could not go anywhere but must remain with only himself to comfort him, wherein lay no hope.

"'I could not flee from myself', he said : 'though I would fain have fled, my loneliness was beyond any human words.'

"And as I listened to this tale", said Socrates, "I remembered how I had heard other things about the companions and the place where the Dead are assembled, and the Blest are accustomed to congregate, and the words of the poet occurred

31

NIGHT AND THE DREAM

to me, as they have doubtless occurred to you who listen to me :

> They came out in a lovely pleasaunce, that dreamed of oases,
> Fortunate isle—the abode of the Blest, that fair happy woodland.
> Here is an ampler sky, those meads are azured by a gentler
> Sun than th' earth, and a new star world their darkness adorneth.

" But I said nothing of this, which may possibly seem strange to you, for I thought possibly this fellow was not ' Blest ', or again, that on these subjects the poet was writing of things of which he had no experience, whereas I was listening to the story of a man who had passed through and returned from this land—and of the two the poet was the less likely to be accurate.

" I will go back to my story. Simonides asked the man who had returned from the Dead why he was so certain that he could have no hope, since he admitted he had never experienced anything like such a place in his life on earth. But the man who returned from the Dead replied that no place on earth could be imagined like the place where he was, but of loneliness in this life he could speak, since once he had been alone on an island near Euboea for several days, being shipwrecked there. And for a few days he had sat upon the beach hoping for a ship to pass by, and being alone he had thoughts upon the

NIGHT AND THE DREAM

Gods and their dealings with men, so that he seemed to become separate and apart from the world, because of the remoteness of the Gods and the uncertainty of their actions, but that when he first awoke in this cold drear place his very soul had become as it were a stranger to him. Neither were there trees, nor the sea as there had been when he was on the island, to remind him of the existence of life around him of which he was a part, nor could even the thought of the Gods comfort him in any way, since they were not, or so it seemed.

" Nor could he obtain comfort in the thought that his evil state was the end, for the vision of even heavier burdens to be laid upon him assailed his soul, and this, together with the fear of what was unseen, and the loneliness, seemed to freeze his soul, and so increasingly terrible was the cold wind that searched and swept the empty corridors of space, stretching for ever around him, that he began to fear that he must perish utterly in this dark and foresaken place. Verily he must have been utterly consumed, he said, for the cold and the loneliness pressed upon him so hard, when of a sudden comfort and warmth came to him in the thought that his present condition, unendurable indeed, must be acceptable to the Gods of the place, since the priests and philosophers had taught him that all places and

NIGHT AND THE DREAM

things were created and conditioned by them, so therefore his fear and intolerable burdens were in some way pleasing to them, or were necessary to his salvation, and as in his earthly life he had suffered grievous things, so too he had been fortunate in others, and it was still his duty to continue as steadfastly as he could, wherever he might be, and thereupon his eyes were opened, and this is what he described.

"'The darkness round me cleared away, and I was before a gateway built in the immensity of space. So high were the pylons that I could see neither the top nor the pediments on which they rested, and I only knew afterwards that it was a gateway, because there was no wind on the further side of the walls, whereas on the side where I was then, there was a great discord of sound which did not cease, and on the one side where my soul was, as it were, born, as once our bodies were born, but in a different way, there was darkness and loneliness and great fear, but on the other side were such things as I shall relate.'

"These were his words and he went on to say that through this gateway neither Time nor Space could come in or go out, but only souls, such as his own, and towards this gateway he felt himself moving, but whether he moved, or whether the gate passed over him, he did not know.

34

NIGHT AND THE DREAM

"But having passed through, the darkness, in which he felt himself enveloped, changed its nature, and become transparent to a light that permeated everything on the other side, but until he changed his position and came to the other side, the darkness comprehended it not.

"This light seemed to warm his soul, so that it could again live and grow, and when he realised that he could partake of life again, but yet in such a different fashion, he knew that he was really dead to the kindly earth, and cut off from all that had been his life aforetime.

"My friend asked him then if he was sorry at having died and having left all such things behind him, to which he replied that so great was the terror and the cold and the loneliness from which he had so shortly escaped that he could not feel sorry at having lost his earthly life which already was behind and was of so little account compared to the misery he had endured outside the gateway, and as for being dead, he was conscious of himself where he was, and in no way felt that his existence was finished, but that rather that certain chapters in the books that were his life had been rolled up, while further rolls still awaited completion, which he himself was destined to write and unroll at the same time.

"The man who came back from the Dead was asked by my friend in what form or shape

35

NIGHT AND THE DREAM

he was, or with what body he was clothed—and it seemed to me a sensible question and even the sort of one I should have asked myself had I been present, and I remembered also the words of the poet who said that we are likely to become 'trailing clouds of glory', so that I listened with some anxiety, especially when I remembered mine own body, hoping that I should not find that the poets were as inaccurate in this matter as they had been in others. To this he replied that when the mists that came from the darkness had cleared away, he saw all around him nothing that in any way resembled the bodies of human persons, or indeed any bodies such as we can conceive, but that on every side of him were spheres of light. These spheres had shape and form and were all of the same pattern, but while each sphere differed the one from the other in colour, all alike were tinted by wreaths of smoke or moving clouds that revolved within them, and that these coils, continually moving, turned the spheres that enclosed them this way and that.

"Such, he said, were the souls of human men in the place where he was. In some way or other he knew that the movement within each sphere was the consciousness of each soul of its own existence, which it could not control or alter, but was of itself. By this I suppose he meant

NIGHT AND THE DREAM

that each soul moved and acted true to itself always, driven or urged by the twisting of the coils within; these coils being themselves and their very essence could not in any way be different from themselves, but must remain for ever the only unchangeable part of man—but I am not sure if I understood this, I can only relate what Simonides told me.

" He said, too, that these spheres could move through and past each other without let or hindrance, but in so passing the coils within each soul were changed afterwards, sometimes in a great degree and sometimes to a very small extent, but in every case the coils of the smoke were altered from the pattern to which aforetime they had been moving.

" In some sort time existed, for, he said, that the movement within the spheres was faster in some than in others, for whereas some moved so slowly within themselves so as to be almost still, others revolved at a great rate, and these spheres especially were influenced by the passing by of the other souls. And as you, Plato, could explain to us, if I were not so occupied in telling you this story, wherever there is harmony, order or proportion, there is also music and colour, so in this place beyond the threshold of death were music and colour also. The spheres differed the one from the other in colour, and in their passage

NIGHT AND THE DREAM

to and fro, were continually changing, but the spheres that seemed to be moving most slowly within themselves retained best the colours with which they had first appeared, and so far from losing the tints with which they were distinguished in their meetings with the other spheres, they became more steadfast, as it were, to their own colours, and even though giving up some of their radiance to others, became more, rather than less, definitely coloured.

"Of Sound he spoke thus. When the wind had gone and the numbness of the outer darkness had passed away, there was an infinity of soft sounds around him. As he got more accustomed to these he could distinguish one note in particular, though that too was sometimes absent.

"Then he noticed that each time he passed through another sphere, he heard two notes more distinctly, but one note was always the same. From this he believed that each Soul in the astral harmony has a number or value which we understand as a note in music.—It would seem that Pythagoras was correct in this,—but I will not argue but rather repeat what I heard.

"Continually then the souls or spheres, acting the one upon the other, moved beyond the gateway towards the greater light beyond, nor could they resist this force that seemed to be drawing all things unto itself. Now he could give no

NIGHT AND THE DREAM

explanation as to this, nor why it should be, or even whence the light came, this much only he knew that the light was outside, or external to themselves, since as they continued their souls became more transparent, and the movements within more definite, and my friend suggested that as the souls became more aware of their existence so the light grew stronger and was external only in that it was manifested outside them.

"But, however this might be, the increase of the light around him enabled him to be the more aware both of the souls around him and his own soul also. And here he said something which interested me very much as it explains many things which I had accepted in my own mind as likely to be the case, but now heard were indeed as I had imagined. I learnt that as the light increased and he was able to look into the souls around him he was thereby enabled to understand his own self better, and how too his life in the body had left its mark, as we say, on his soul.

"For some of the spheres were so dark that he was scarcely able to see the whorls within them. Such souls as these, he said, were tinted and dyed with the desires of their lost bodies, others again had not the glass or crystal-like appearance which some souls possessed for the surface was, as it were, 'scratched', and that was the word he used, with fine lines that did not change,

NIGHT AND THE DREAM

and these lines hampered their progress and caused them to lag behind the smoother spheres.

"These continuous movements of one sphere relative to the others were not 'progress' as we understand it on earth, for he would continually stop to try and explain that there was movement neither forward nor backward, nor faster nor slower, nor upwards nor down. Time too was absent from this place, for he could not explain how long he spent in the journeyings he made, nor how much of our earthly time was expended in this phase or that of his experiences.

"This much only would he say, 'Beyond the threshold there is neither time nor space as we understand it, but I was aware of all things that happened to me, one thing following another, and I could remember both my life on earth and my life in this place. I remembered the coldness and the terror which first laid hands upon me, before the gates were passed, and the beginning of light coming through the darkness. As I approached the light, or it may be as the light approached nearer to me, the terrors I had been through and had in some sort overcome, became part of my very being and were absorbed into my soul—so that I now know that these were in no wise worthy of fear, but were occasioned by my substance yet being imperfect.'

"When I heard this last phrase I asked the

40

NIGHT AND THE DREAM

man who had watched in the temple, if his friend had been a philosopher, since several of the words he used were common indeed among such as were learned in philosophy, but not to the ordinary citizen, but he told me 'no'. Then, I said, my story telling friend you at any rate have been a student of these things, and he answered me 'yes'.

"But to continue my tale. The man who returned from the Dead (I never learnt his name) said that his increasing knowledge of the souls around him brought home to him the certainty that he was not in a Dream (from which in any case his former terror must have awakened him) but was, indeed, dead, and together with these others in the place of departed spirits. Nor did the knowledge of his condition then make him sad or sorry as being without hope, but rather glad, since the stories that he had heard, and had yet hardly believed, were now proved true, in that life or consciousness persisted after the body had perished, yet at the same time he was apprehensive what further trials awaited him.

"Already he knew that there must be such experiences, for his soul was growing, and as the life he had lived on the earth was continually changing as his body grew older, so he reasoned would his soul in its growth feel new sensations. So thinking, he wondered whether he might

NIGHT AND THE DREAM

meet with some soul that aforetime he had known as a friend, or even as an enemy, who having passed over unto death before him, might comfort or prepare his soul for what might lie in his path, never thinking, he said, that such companionship would hinder him, and with such thoughts he remembered especially the last men he had seen, and the wounds that his body had received when he had been surprised by the slaves in the wood.

"It was this that reminded him that he was no longer hindered as he had been before, now that his body was gone with all its hunger and thirst, appetite and desire, so that he could even rejoice to be rid of it, as a man on earth rejoices when some great trouble has passed him by."

Socrates paused for a moment:

"You who are listening to me now will remember the account handed down to us of the descent of Ulysses, while yet alive, into Hades, and how he raised up with dark blood the shades of those whom he had known aforetime. It seems to me that we should rejoice likewise that the poet was inaccurate in this—for my part I should not like my life after death to be disturbed by idle questionings from those we have left behind.

"Simonides said that he asked how or in what way he could remember such things since his mortal body was no longer with him, and he

42

NIGHT AND THE DREAM

replied that it was true that although he was without a body as we understand it, he could remember, not only everything he had ever done, but all persons whom he had ever met, whether they were friends, or parents, or lovers, or enemies. He could not explain in any way why these things were so, but he insisted that what had happened to him in his former life was more vivid and real to him now that he had gone away, than when he had been alive, and memories of his childhood were as intense as events which had befallen him a week before he had died, and further, that many things which he had long forgotten had come back, as it were, into his memory.

" So that his whole life, and not only the events, but his very thoughts, had become part and parcel of the sphere which he knew was himself, for it had been built up in his former life, in outline at least, by everything that had befallen him.

" In some such way as this he tried to explain how these things should be so. All his life aforetime, he said, had been governed by a Cause or Law, of which he had not been conscious or even suspected, but nevertheless it was the necessity of obeying this Law that had made his life as it had been, and all that had befallen him had followed as a direct consequence of the working out of this Law among other souls and bodies situated similar to his own.

43

NIGHT AND THE DREAM

"What he had thought to be but the blind working of chance, or the malicious interference of some irresponsible deity, was but the fulfilment of his Law working in its varying occasions. This Law, he said, was the same for all created things and persons born into this world, and for other things also, but that it manifested itself in different forms of matter in what seemed different ways, but the difference was not genuine, while the varying manifestation of the Law in varying forms or shapes or bodies caused that flow of events or change for which we, too, are accustomed to blame the Goddess or the Fates or even Fortune. Under the operation of this Law he had been born into the world, at the time and amid the surroundings suitable to his condition, but that was not for him the first fulfilment of the Law, but rather his first manifestation on this earth under the Law, nor could he escape from the workings of this Law in any way now that he was dead.

"And sometimes he called this Law 'Life' using the same word, and sometimes he called it the 'Unseen Force' or 'Cause'.

"When he understood that he was still bound to the Girdle of Necessity, or the Law that was his being, and that this same Law still retained the same power over his future that it had exercised over his past, his courage returned to

NIGHT AND THE DREAM

him yet the more, so that he was the more anxious to approach nearer to the Light which he began to associate with the Law or Cause of his being, and that seemed to beckon him on, bidding him to undertake the future with a light heart, as it promised him greater fullness of life. And here my friend asked him how he could talk about the future and what he meant thereby since he had said that time was not in the place wherein he found himself—to which he replied that he was unable to explain how this should be, but it was clear enough to him there, but when back again in this life he would not understand it so well, but that all the same it was as he said. He would repeat that ' Yonder ' things known and realised were the past or the present, things not understood were the future, and that, for them, neither past, present or future, could hinder the Soul or limit their activities, and that an increased consciousness of reality enabled them to surpass the bounds of Time, what he then understood and was conscious of was the past, what he did not know was the future, and the present was not.

" Saying this he told them as he learnt the Laws of the place and began to comprehend the things he had tried to explain, and that the limitations of his life on earth could no longer bind or fetter his soul, the Light was able to penetrate into his innermost being with more

NIGHT AND THE DREAM

power, but when he tried to rely on the recollection of his human earthly mind or reason, doubts and misunderstandings came like clouds between him and the light, so that he seemed to be receding from the haven where he fain would be.

" Then did he realise that since his five senses had left him, as faithful slaves no longer able to protect his house, the sphere that was his soul, and indeed all that remained of the self he knew, must entertain the Light or likewise die. In this Light was food for his soul whereby alone he might continue to exist, and what air and food had been to his body aforetime, and what poetry and music had been to his mind, so now this Light sustained his soul and kept it alive and in being, since his soul could in no wise exist by itself, but like his body on the earth must rely on things external to itself. So that it would seem, said Socrates, as if the Soul is not in any way Immortal by itself, but must depend on the same source of Life and Power which had manifested itself in the earthly life as growth, depending on food for the body and food for the mind, and in the next life manifested itself as food for the Soul. Knowing this, he was the more able to read and understand the Souls that surrounded and accompanied him on his journey.

" He read them without pride or regret or pity, but rather with understanding and sympathy,

NIGHT AND THE DREAM

in that they too, like himself, were fast bound in the coils of an All-powerful Law or Cause. He went on to say that he could find no difference between the souls of Greeks and Barbarians, nor were the souls of slaves different in any respect from the souls of free men, which is perhaps difficult for us to understand. In some souls he could see great joy in that they had been freed from a grievous burden of physical pain that had so short a time ago been continually with them, on the other hand in others, great sorrow because they had been snatched away from the earth without the clash of arms, or the sufferings of some grievous sickness to soften or loosen the bonds which naturally bind men to this mortal life of ours. Others again, were still sad at heart because devouring love for their dear ones, still alive, held them back to the chains of earth, notwithstanding that they had the means of bringing the presence of those they loved within their consciousness—these and such as these were the most impervious to the Light, since it was inevitable that any affection for the life that had been, in that place Yonder was a hindrance rather than a help in approaching the Light, which alone was powerful in that place.

" To which my friend that told me the story asked in what form or guise the earth and its inhabiters appeared. He was told that as life

NIGHT AND THE DREAM

that was past was still so much part of the Soul as the life of the Future was inherent in the Soul itself, neither the one nor the other could be separated or torn out of the soul or the laws of its being, and that there was no difficulty in recalling any incident of the life of earth. For all that had happened to the soul was the necessary sequence of the Law operating in the flesh, and under earthly conditions, and as such could be recalled at will, as a chain may be retraced link by link, but that these memories (if they were memories and not real and actual facts) were flat and without depth, very much as pictures painted on the temple walls only seemed to be in relief, whereas the conditions of his celestial life stood out, like the sculptures on a frieze, this was the actual comparison he used to explain what he meant.

" When again his hearers pressed him to explain the absence of Time or Space Yonder, he could only reply that although such things might appear to be real in the life on earth, Yonder they had neither importance nor reality, nor could they fetter the soul as they had once appeared to limit or control the body.

" Before he could approach nearer, as he so earnestly desired, to the Light that he knew sustained him, so that he could ' live more fully '—and these again were his very words—he felt again the

NIGHT AND THE DREAM

breath of a cold and bitter wind, but this time coming from himself, in that he regretted bitterly what things he had done, or refrained from doing, in defiance of the Law that had been and still was his being. He went on to explain that this Law has each one of us encompassed with bounds that we may not pass, never the less in all men was the power given at birth, not so much to defy, as to act in a contrary fashion to, the Law, and that this power or choice to choose one of two ways, notwithstanding the power of the Law of our being, enable mortal men to act, sometimes it may be without meaning it, in opposition to the Law. The effect of such actions could not in any way prevent the fulfilment of the Law, but it was possible to deflect the course of our lives slightly, as it were, from a straight line. And in larger bodies of men acting together, some similar deflection might be made in the Life of the City or the State, since each collective body of men must obey, in the long run, he said, the Collective Law which existed for such bodies as it did for the individual.

" Knowing then that he himself had acted in this manner, and that many times, even sometimes when he was doing what seemed good deeds and as such acceptable to the Gods, he was exceeding sorrowful, having failed to run his course straight. But comfort came to him,

49

NIGHT AND THE DREAM

he said, in this way. His remorse for his failings was born of himself and caused the outer texture of his soul to soften so that the air (for such he described it well knowing that it was not air) could enter and penetrate to the innermost parts of his being. But this may have been due to the activities that were powerful around him, and which varied from one place in Heaven to another, since he noticed that the other spheres that were his companions had become clear to his view at the same time and place, and he believed that the Soul after Death passes through as it were, bands or belts of spiritual food, and that these, each in their own degree and habit, affect the soul in various ways, so in his own experience courage or remorse or hope alternately prevailed upon his soul as it journeyed towards the Light.

" Now I suppose that you who are listening ", said Socrates, " will want to ask me many and searching questions—indeed I can see it in the way you listen—but remember I can only relate to you the tale as I have heard it. Of a truth I confess I asked many questions of my friend, and such of these that he could answer I have incorporated in the Story of the Man who returned from the Dead.

" One question in particular I was anxious to ask, for having read the official stories, that those, who alone claim to have correct information in

NIGHT AND THE DREAM

these matters, tell of their existence in this other place,—You will remember their description of judgment—' of the just decrees of Rhadamanthus whom father Cronos has for a perpetual colleague ' stories of fantastic and horrible early Gods and the like,—so I was anxious to know which of the Immortals were visible, and also if they were doing the kind of things which they have been accused of doing, I mean in particular, drinking wine and quarrelling among themselves, or if, on the other hand, these and such like amusements were no longer congenial to the dwellers on Olympus.

"As you may expect, some such questions my friend had asked. This was the reply from the man who had witnessed—that he could not see any that resembled Zeus the Deliverer, or any other god-like persons, nor could he find any doing such things as the Immortals are supposed to enjoy, and he went so far as to say that he saw no mountains either, for which I, at any rate, am glad, for although at certain times mountains are beautiful, the Plains of Attica seem to me to be as desirable as any place, either now or then.

"But to continue my tale. My friend, who had been present when first this story was told in the temple, was able to help me with my enquiries, for, having himself attended the Festival of Eleusis—he had witnessed the masque

51

NIGHT AND THE DREAM

of Death, the Arena of Judgment, and the Punishment of the Wicked. And although he had not been sufficiently instructed or proficient to attend that last Mystery wherein is disclosed to the initiated what joys await the Virtuous in the Second Life, he was able to ask many questions which were pertinent to these matters, but since I had not been initiated, unfortunately, he could not tell me how near to the truth the priests of Eleusis had been—but as regards the exceeding great joy which the souls of the Departed experience when first the Light takes them into itself, he was able to say this—' When I was at Thebes, I lodged in the house of a flax worker called Semeria and I became her lover. She it was who brought me to the feasts of Isis, who is a Goddess of great power and manifold enchantments for those who dwell by the banks of the Nile. To the mysteries of Isis I was also initiated, and after many trials of endurance, and having passed the necessary tests, those of us who had been accepted by the priests were taken by night into her Temple. Of much that happened there I may not speak, but I can never forget the joy I felt, which far exceeded anything that I had before known, when the priest, clothed in black, after having said the favourable words, standing before the altar—the temple being in absolute darkness, said ' Behold I show you

NIGHT AND THE DREAM

the Mystery ' and straightway the curtains were rolled back, and the Goddess disclosed to us in a blaze of light. I felt that I was indeed part of the Goddess who had received me into herself, and such knowledge is too deep and high for any words to express and must be learnt in some such way as this, before it can be understood.

" So spake Simonides, the man who had watched beside the bier, and it is for you, my friends, to understand. But let us go back to the actual events that had befallen the soul of his friend. As his soul came nearer to the Light, he began to realise how much he was eaten up with desire to become one with the Light, as the lover desires to become one with his beloved, when he saw before him a deep chasm opening out in space between him and the Light on the farther side. So deep was this chasm that the Light which was everywhere around him could not penetrate to the black shadows of the deeps, and ceased to be, for he could watch the spheres, having wavered a little, hovering to and fro, slowly descend before him, getting more and more dim as the light ceased to sustain them in their descent into the black pit. He knew that in spite of his desire to become one with the Light, he was but after all in the outer Courtyard of the Justice of the Law, and that in order to gain the Abode of Justice, it was his bounden duty to enter into the

NIGHT AND THE DREAM

darkness which thrust itself, as it were, before his path, even if it should mean that he must of himself give over his soul unto death.

" But since he said that his human nature was not entirely put away from him, he was not desirous of further trials of his hope and his endurance, now that they were actually in front of him, but would rather, he thought, stay where he was, but that this could not be, as he felt himself, so far from remaining in that place, receding from the Light and going back towards the Outer Darkness. And straightway it seemed worse to him then to lose the Light and his desire to become part of the Light itself, than in his former existence on earth had been his dread of deformity or Death. He knew too that his soul cried out for the Light even more than his body had cried out for Life, so that he felt that he was wasting his time not to enter upon, and that immediately, such trials or dangers as came in his path, and rather than become unworthy of beholdin g such visions as might be in store, he too, cast his troubled and trembling soul into the blackness of the pit. And this pit he would call the Trial of the Endurance of the Soul, in that it was always possible for him to return if he had willed it, but that having determined to take what came in his path, he continued in his descent into the pit. As the walls seemed to

NIGHT AND THE DREAM

pass upwards all that remained to him of earth was winnowed out of him—at other times he would say burnt out of him rather than winnowing—but he would go on to explain, not burning as we burn the bodies of the Dead, for that destroys flesh and bones and leaves only ashes, but rather a cleansing fire that could only purge away what was of the earth, earthy, and could not effect, much less destroy, the spirit or the soul.

" And as part of himself seemed to vanish, but without pain, or any sense of loss such as accompanies our earthly ills, so there passed from out his soul any desire to excel either in virtue or in any other way. For, he said that in the place where he was, nothing was more foreign than a lack of proportion, or as we should say, it was above all things necessary to view his existence with moderation, and that when this lack of proportion, from which we mortals suffer so much, had been replaced by a fair and just view of both his position in the scheme of things both mortal and Immortal, then it was he knew himself as an Immortal Soul ; being without value to others, without weight, or position, or indeed being without any attribute at all, except in so far as he could bear witness to the Light, which like an eagle descending, came to him from the realms above into the darkness of the pit, which was the endurance of his soul.

55

NIGHT AND THE DREAM

"And he explained that this Light was but parcel of himself, and yet was of a divine nature, being part of eternity, or God, or whatever other name philosophers give to the Life Force manifesting itself in our mortal nature. No reproaches, he said, did his Immortal Soul utter to his earthly soul, for his Immortal Soul knew itself to be tied down, as it were, to his earthly soul, and bound up with its destiny, just as his earthly soul had been bound to the body that he had left behind such a short time ago. It being the burden of necessity in our Divine Nature that as the body partook of three persons or identities, so too the soul must divide into three portions, and as the first body must in due time be burnt and returned back to the Elements from which it had laboriously been built up, so too the earthly soul must be purified until the God-like principle, remaining true to itself and freed of all corruption, can fly again like a dove back to its creator and Mother, which is the Divine Principle and from which it had drawn its existence.

"With some such words as these, my friends, my story is done, for the watchers in the Temple having seen the body of the man stir on the bier, they put warm clothes on his feet and body, and having rubbed his heart and hands with wine and oil, after a long time, with many sighs and groanings, and in much travail, his body left

NIGHT AND THE DREAM

that country yonder of which we fain would know more, and returned to this life of ours.

" It would seem that the Immortals have set many and great obstacles in our way lest we find out the geography (shall we say) of this place, for they put the price of our knowledge of these things very high—at least it seems so to us, for the lowest price that we can offer, and that they will accept, is the death of our bodies.

" But I have finished now, having told you the tale as I heard it. You will agree with me that it concerns such things as you have been speaking about."

Now when Socrates had told us the tale which I have just repeated for you as accurately as I can remember, another silence fell upon our company, no one wishing to say anything which would break the spell which his words had cast upon us.

Plato it was who spoke first, and turning over towards Socrates, for he had been turned away from him while the story had been told, he said, " You are still at your old profession Socrates. Once a mid-wife, I suppose always a mid-wife. You know you have only told us this in order to extract from us, somehow or other, what we think of your story, in order that you may tell us that we really mean something else. But I will meet you with your own weapons and will ask you a

57

NIGHT AND THE DREAM

question, that is if you are not too tired of talking, and will answer me willingly."

" Certainly I will answer your question, if I can that is, for some of you may ask me such things that I cannot answer."

" Well then, Socrates, do you believe yourself in this story that you have told us ? "

" I must believe in my own stories—for one thing—you have all listened to me so patiently I can be certain that it has entertained you, as it entertained me when I heard it."

Plato was smiling at this when Critias burst in : " No, what Plato means is this, Socrates—was it a true story that you told us, and did such things as we have heard, really happen to anyone who verily seemed to die, and afterwards returned to the earth to tell of his adventures ? "

Before Socrates could reply Plato spoke for himself :

" No doubt I may have asked such a question when in my own good time and after much labour I had achieved that grasp of things which came so much more readily to Critias. But rather than you should deem me too slow, I will not persist, but ask you something else. Do you believe, Socrates, that this dream—if you will allow the word—is a true representation, or Idea of that Life Yonder in which some of us believe ? "

NIGHT AND THE DREAM

To which Socrates replied as follows, speaking more seriously than was his usual custom, in fact I believe that was the first time, and indeed the last, that I ever saw him so.

" All my life, my friends, I have been puzzling over the problems of the Life that shall be, when the soul has left the body. Before I had heard of this experience of a mortal man who had been caught up into Heaven, several things had occurred to me as being likely to happen.

" As to the shape or body that we shall enjoy Yonder, or the place, or the geography, as I said, I am content to believe that what has happened to one man may equally well happen to another. In my ignorance, one thing seemed to me certain, that the presence of friends and companions would be as necessary for my happiness after Death, as it is in this present life. This it seems is not so. Another thing I had imagined that we should certainly meet with the Gods, not indeed as the poets have told us, as a band of revellers but as a company of divine companions, who would succour us and help us to become more divine. Perhaps I have depended too much on this also, as on the Idea of companionship.

" Now I can no longer think that the mountain of Heaven is either Here or There, Now or Then, and however high we may fly into the air, or descend into the earth or the sea, it will be

59

NIGHT AND THE DREAM

impossible for us to say Here or There is Heaven, on the other hand we cannot say with any more certainty that Heaven is not Here and Now, it may be in this very room. No doubt when the knocking on the door announces for us each in our turn that Death bids us away, we may think differently—but at this present moment I can believe that what I have told you, or at any rate, something like it, is true of our Immortal Life.

" If this Life which we now enjoy is to end at Death, it will still be needful for us to live so that we may obtain the happiness which is within our power to retain, but if on the other hand only part of us will survive and go on existing somewhere and somehow, may we not expect that it will be that the part of our mind which seeks after eternal things is the most likely to be able to continue. For like things go the like. Drinking and eating and loving, shall I add, talking, will perish with all the turmoil of the desires and passions that belong to the body. We know this also from experience—that in our own bodies Nature takes from us such of her good things that we no longer care about— or perhaps it is because we no longer care about them that Nature takes them away—but we do not seem to lose in the same way that searching out after the things of the spirit, for as we get older

NIGHT AND THE DREAM

such things increase rather than diminish in importance. May we not say that the search for such things is a sign that we are alive to the things of the spirit, and that therefore something exists in us which must persist and survive death. And if for some, such things are no longer of interest, and we all know of some to whom this would apply, then these, though their bodies are still alive, are in respect of immortal life, dead. As for me, 'By the Dog' eternity has always seemed both Here and Now, if we would only have the courage to try and partake of her.

" Even the coldness of Death may be overcome in this life while we yet breathe, if we hold fast to the Heavenly vision that is within and around us.

" And if we are enabled, by so ruling our earthly life, that we are continually seeking those things which are the image of the Heavenly, to so partake of this, the shadow of the things that shall be—why then, when in due time Death himself overtakes us as we travel on our journey Heavenwards, we shall hand over to him our earthly garments, since he will demand them and will not be refused, and we can continue along the same road without restraint, and not entirely as strangers—leaving behind us such things as Death demands, to do with them as he

NIGHT AND THE DREAM

will, since they are no longer of any value to our souls."

As Socrates said these words, the first touch of Saffron-Gowned Dawn was laid on the pillars of Agathon's porch, and knowing that the Day had come we arose, and having said that Hymn to Apollo that begins : " O glorious Apollo we come fresh from the perils of darkness, grant that any words we have heard this night be no longer harmful : and let us now go forth to another day with thy shield ever before us ", we set out each for his own home. This was the last time I saw Socrates.

THE VERDICT

THE VERDICT

For Mine enemies speak against me, and they that lay wait for my Soul take their counsel together, saying, God hath forsaken him, persecute him, and take him, for there is none to deliver him.—*Psalm* lxxi. 9.

CHARACTERS

Neoptolemus	–	A rich Athenian
Clinias	– –	The Host
Eryxias	– –	An Athenian citizen
Archion	– –	A Soldier
Neiridion	– –	A Sailor
Anytus	– –	An Accuser of Socrates
Meletus	– –	,, ,, ,,
Aristogiton	–	A young man
Aristophanes	–	The Playwright
Diotimus	–	A Stranger

NEOPTOLEMUS is speaking

THE VERDICT

You must not ask me to believe in political justice. For one thing I have lived too long in this City to believe in anything, and for another I was present when the Trial of the Generals took place, and also at the Trial of Socrates that followed seven years afterwards.

I was old enough to record my vote at this, and I can assure you I took a very serious view of the importance of my decision, but looking back, I am not at all certain that Justice was served either by the decision of my fellow citizens in general, or my vote in particular.

Should you ever go to the theatre and see the old masterpieces performed, you would rightly feel emotion at the time, but, when safely home again, you would remember the excellence of the actor rather than the sufferings of the hero.

I will tell you what was said in the House of Clinias that same night after the trial was over, and Socrates had been committed to the House of the Eleven, and you shall form your own opinion as to the Justice of it.

I know that the story of the death of the hero, or the chief actor, which ever expression

THE VERDICT

you prefer, has been recorded by a great artist, and one who never allowed either his readers or himself to forget that reason should be tinged with emotion, but my art is not that of the playwright, though the discussion partook of both Tragedy and Comedy as you will hear, but rather that of the remembrancer.

You young men, did not have the advantages of our system of education, you were not compelled from your earliest years, aided by the rod, to recite The "Wrath of Achilles" and other masterpieces, so that you have not the memory which we had perforce to acquire, nor have you the gift of happy quotation which is the mark, as the goldsmiths say, of an Athenian Scholar.

As I have told you, I spent the whole day in the Assembly listening to the speeches, but after the judges had delivered their sentence, it was so late in the evening, that I went away, for I had promised Clinias that I would dine at his house. Being quite near the steps, I got out quickly, and was some way down the hill when Clinias himself, walking much faster than his wont, overtook me. Even in those days Clinias was inclined to be fat and hurrying downhill made him short of breath, so he could only pant as he passed: "I am expecting you—Aristophanes refuses to come." The absence of Aristophanes will leave an empty place, I thought, and as I

THE VERDICT

wondered who would be deemed worthy or willing to come at such short notice, I heard another man behind me, and who should I see but the playwright himself.

Aristophanes would also have passed me without a word, but I spoke to him: "Our dinner will be quite spoilt for Clinias tells me that you are not coming to-night." He peered up at me, with his head on one side like a saucy sparrow, and then making up his mind to speak, he ejaculated: "True, Neoptolemus"; and having taken a few steps at my pace he continued in his dryest vein: "I, also, have an oracle, who has spoken to me, and he bids me be alone." Thinking to please him I said: "We have both seen a great drama to-day, and perhaps you wish to record what is fresh in your memory. If I was a playwright, no doubt I should feel the same." But my words, harmless enough you would think, enraged him, for he said: "If you were a writer, you would not say such things, nor would you think as you do", and before I could reply he hurried on.

The boy, who was carrying my chair, was too far away from me to have annoyed him, and many times before going to sleep I have composed suitable and adequate replies to his speech, but I always console myself for saying nothing at the time by remembering that Aristophanes

69

THE VERDICT

was a dangerous man with whom to bandy words, so I walked alone to my house and roused my slaves, none too kindly, for I will admit I was in a bad temper.

After my bath I was completely restored, and I took especial delight in being shaved, for one thing, it would have annoyed Aristophanes so much. Hot water, and oil and the right selection of scent produce a feeling of virtue, which, in my opinion is more often derived from getting rid of evil (and after all dust is an evil) than merely doing virtuous things. In fact I was so completely restored to my usual genial good humour, that not even the appearance of Eryxias, also on his way to the house of Clinias, could disturb me.

" I do not think that any of you can remember Eryxias as he died very soon after the events of which I speak, but in the Sicilian War he served in the army of Nicias, and was one of those unfortunates surrounded in the olive garden of Polyzalus and sold into the stone quarries of Achradina. Having a strong body he escaped with his life, but with little else.

For some reason he was persuaded that the Goddess herself had come to his rescue, and as a sort of return he vowed himself to her service for the rest of his life. This, as I said, was fortunately short, for neither party, if I may say so, were gainers by the bargain, nor can I

THE VERDICT

personally ever believe that the Goddess had inter-
fered personally on his behalf, for Eryxias in no
way resembled Odysseus, for example, or indeed
anyone but himself, nevertheless he believed in
the whole thing, and retaining both his obsession
and his vows, was to be found in the precincts
of the temple by day or night, and in time, I
have no doubt he would have acquired some
official post in the ceremonies, but for his voice,
which being small and reedy, made him even
more ridiculous.

As you can imagine all these disasters falling
on one never renowned for intelligence or moderation, made him rather a nuisance than a pleasant
companion, nor were the things he was accustomed
to say always suited to his company, so that many
treated him as a madman, and indeed his sufferings
in Syracus were cruel beyond measure.

At any rate it was with such a one that I
walked to the House of Clinias, and on the way
he thought fit to regale me with an account,
in some detail, of a quarrel among his fellows.
As far as I can remember it had been proposed
that the Robes of the Statue carried in the Pana-
thenæa should be lengthened but it might have
been shortened, in any case it seemed to Eryxias a
serious matter. I was myself more concerned
with the names of those who were to be of our
company that night.

THE VERDICT

Thus we arrived, my companion still piping his protests like Pan, to find the company assembled. Archion, the soldier, Neiridion whom I had not seen since Arginusæ, two of the orators of the day, Anytus, quiet but triumphant and Meletus triumphant but not quiet, and Aristogiton a youth of great beauty and even greater wealth, to whom Antisthenes the banker had bequeathed the greater part of his vast fortune. The presence of these, some of whom were my friends, reconciled me to the proximity of Eryxias, so that I could sympathise with him almost cheerfully under the trouble which was overwhelming him, though, as I said, I never fully understood what he was talking about.

I noticed that as usual nine couches, one for each of the Muses, had been prepared, and Clinias interpreted my glance. "Aristophanes" he said, "but he will not come." I should have asked Socrates, had he been acquitted, but since the Fates have decided otherwise, an empty place will remind us all of our mortality—and his fate, therefore, let us enjoy ourselves as far as we can ; we are not women that we should cry aloud if one of our number is taken away."

With these words we took our places, and it was not without care that I placed myself as far as possible from Eryxias.

When the flute players had finished the first

THE VERDICT

music, I turned to our host : "Clinias", I said, "You have gathered a rare company to-night and it would be a great pity if anything trivial or unworthy was the subject of our conversation, but since you have here two of the victors in the Assembly to-day, would it not be well if we talked of the trial, it being understood that neither Meletus nor Anytus repeated those speeches which we have already heard." "Certainly", he said, ' if that is agreeable to you all.'

But Archion dissented, saying : "It is true that I was not present at this trial, but I am told that our friends spoke for two hours apiece, so that it is impossible for them to have anything fresh to add, even if they are not hoarse."

Neiridion was on his side too, for he spoke at once. "I am not certain that we have any occasion for rejoicing in this matter. The action of the Assembly in my opinion does no credit to this City, and will not bear looking into. For some of us were the friends of Socrates and loved him too dearly to enjoy hearing people say :

Ay me, wise Peleus Son, very bitter tidings must thou hear,
Such as I would have never been.
Fallen is Patroklus, and they are fighting round his body naked."

After this, it was impossible for Clinias to continue the subject in harmony so that the flute players began again, playing very sweetly.

73

THE VERDICT

All the while I was thinking how we could bring in the subject of the day's trial, but without avail, when something happened which decided the matter finally.

The front doors had been barred for fear lest some wandering revellers should disturb the company, so we heard nothing of the world outside until the voices of strangers came from the garden.

Clinias got up, for such could only come from the bearers of ill tidings, or someone who was familiar with the household, but when he reached the garden entrance we could see Aristophanes and with him a stranger. With that gift for happy quotation, which I still claim is the product of our classical education, Clinias turned to his new guests, declaiming:

"As when a man whom spite of Fate hath cursed in his own land for homicide, that he flieth abroad and seeketh asylum with some Lord, and they that see him are filled with amazement. Even so now Achilles was amazed, as he saw Priam enter, and the men all were amazed, and looked upon each other in terror."

But Aristophanes paused only to complete the quotation—"But Priam as Hermes hath bade, bow'd down to beseech him. This I do also Clinias, since I owe you an apology, first for refusing to come, and then breaking in upon

THE VERDICT

your company. But since I left you this after-
noon, the Gods have been kind to me. Not that
I am guilty of homicide, as yet, nor am I searching
for the fallen body of a friend, for I know where
my friends spend their nights, but Hermes,
no less, has sent to me a stranger from Eos,
Diotimus the Son of Gryllus, who having long
heard of the virtue that abides always in the City
of the Violet Crown, has risked many things on
his journey here, in order that he may meet with
those most acquainted with virtue. For quite
different qualities, I must presume, he came
to my house, but learning of his desires, I have
brought him here where virtue and knowledge
are ever to be found, and more especially about this
time."

Some of the company looked very pleased at
this, especially Aristogiton who was young enough
to be deceived with the soft beginnings of such a
speech, then the playwright continued : " In
the house of Clinias, O Diotimus, you are meeting
all that remains of virtue in Athens. Let me
introduce you ! A sailor without a ship, a
warrior without a command, a soldier who has
tasted of slavery, two of our foremost orators,
a rich youth, a man of the world, a poor playwright, and the cultured but portly gentleman
at whose feast we are assembled. It is your
misfortune that you cannot talk to the most

THE VERDICT

virtuous man of our City, but he is not available to-night, since his fellow citizens have to-day sent him to the House of the Eleven, and the gaoler will not permit us to enter—as guests—after sundown."

All this time Diotimus, who was a typical Islander, was standing waiting his chance of speaking to Clinias, and saying something elegant or apposite to convince us that the islanders were after all civilised people, but so many names uttered, the one after the other seemed to confuse him, and it was almost with a start that he found Clinias speaking to him. " You are doubly welcome Diotimus to this house and this company, firstly because you come from Eos, and secondly, in that you have brought Aristophanes with you. As you will learn to-night, his presence makes us all—shall I say—at our best. Come sit by me, and ask for what you will, but if you have already eaten join with us in drinking."

As both the new comers had already dined, figs were brought in with fresh wine, and after we had said such prayers as were suitable or sufficient, we asked Diotimus in turn what things he had seen in our City that seemed to him of the greatest interest, and each of us, as far as our special knowledge would permit, enlightened him answering his questions.

This gave me the chance I had long been

76

THE VERDICT

seeking, and when it came to my turn, I said :
" O Diotimus, such things as temples and Statues
may be seen in many cities, nor do I doubt that
your island also could show such beautiful
buildings as would make us jealous, but to-day,
before the whole Assembly the people of Athens
have made trial and condemned to death, one
of our most famous citizens, the like of which I
do not think you can have seen in any other City
in Hellas. If therefore you were a witness of that
trial, it would interest us all to know how such
a thing impressed a Greek, although not of our
blood ? " To this the stranger Diotimus, replied
as follows, in the somewhat laboured and flowery
style which passes for courtesy or culture among
those beyond the sea.

" I deem it a great honour, Men of Athens, to
find myself at last in your great City, but especially do I prize my presence at this banquet. I
can assure you that for many years to come your
names, gentlemen, will be familiar to my country-
men. In my land, we have long envied the
supremacy of your City, both in Art and Laws,
nor need I remind you of the sympathy we showed
and the perils we shared at your side in the Great
War." He paused at this point sufficiently
long for me to look at Archion, to see how he
would take such a tribute to an island which,
it was notorious, achieved great wealth by

THE VERDICT

trading both with Athens and Sparta, while sending a few hoplites and two ill-found vessels to the fleet, but he merely looked under his eyebrows at the orator who continued.

" Although we can claim Kinship with you, our history is too short for us to have produced those masterpieces of antiquity which we so greatly envy. Sirs, you have an atmosphere, which, if we could, we would copy, since neither buildings nor statues can procure that tradition of mellowed age which we so especially appreciate in our walks through your streets." As he paused again for breath, or for fresh adjectives, Aristophanes glanced round the table, and sighed so loudly that I wondered if the solitary meal to which he had looked forward in the morning had been exorcised by this garrulous but benevolent visitor; I could quite understand now why he had thought it fairer to share with others the abundance of good things that Hermes had sent him.

The stranger from Eos went on : " Each of the Cities and States I have seen has evolved for itself a code of conduct peculiar to itself, but through them all, and in despite of every variety of detail, runs the Greek genius, if I may so style it. This genius expresses itself, I find, best in the service of the Gods and in the operation of the Laws, so that it is my custom to seek first the Law Courts everywhere I go."

THE VERDICT

"Did you hear it all?", I asked him, for I thought we should be listening all night, and after all the fellow could not expect us to weigh every word he uttered. "I heard the whole of the trial", he replied; "having been given a seat, I was present at the opening speech and I heard the last words of the accused."

Clinias leaned forward: "It would be a great privilege, Diotimus, if you would continue; as Athenians we view to-day as quite an event in our times, but to find in our midst one who can speak from experience, and tell us how far our especial troubles effect to that Greek ideal which you have traced, is a privilege and an education to us all."

"To tell the truth", said Diotimus, "I was so exalted at finding myself in your Assembly, that I did not hear, or rather I did not follow, the first speech for the prosecution—although I was much impressed, as were all around me, by the eloquence and agility of the speaker.

"Poetry is not considered of the first importance in Eos, so that I was rather at sea, as we say, to understand what quarrel modern poets can have with their traducers."

"But what did you think of the arguments of the second orator", asked Aristophanes, while I watched the face of Anytus who was setting his features in advance so as not to appear either mortified or self-conscious.

THE VERDICT

"It seemed to me that such serious accusations were not supported by evidence that was conclusive", was the reply. "At home", said the stranger, " I have often listened to the charge of corrupting youth being brought against many of our citizens, a charge easy to bring, but very difficult to prove, since at best a youth is merely a youth until he has been corrupted, then he becomes a man, and that after all is the destiny of youth. But we have never proceeded against anyone for introducing new deities or scorning the observances. So serious a charge is inconceivable without the most ample evidence—and yet nothing very definite on this head was produced against this malefactor of yours, at least nothing that seemed conclusive to me."

" It is ill to offend a stranger ", began Meletus, and his harsh voice and dour looks were too remarkable even for the stranger not to realise that one of the orators of the day was speaking, " but in this City at any rate, the suspicion of impiety is held an accursed thing. The Athenians have from earliest times been famous for their devotion to our Lady."

Here Eryxias coughed loudly endeavouring to impress the stranger, presumably, for he could not succeed with us—"consequently," continued the orator, " there is no crime which we hold so heinous as attempts to subvert morals or endanger the worship of the Goddess.

THE VERDICT

"Let me tell you—and his harsh voice became strident—we have not thought it beneath our dignity to drive into exile even Anaxagoras—in his day, the most famous philosopher in all Hellas —for attempting to propagate impious doctrines, nor have we witheld our hand," and here he raised his own, "from the household of our greatest statesman, and that in the prime of his power, because forsooth, impiety lay at his right hand. And I would add this Diotimus, so long as Athens, or indeed any City, remains pious and orthodox in her religion, so long will she remain Sacred and Secure, but as soon as the voice of the innovator, or the wiles of the atheist—"

"I thought that to-day's speeches were forbidden", said Archion, who could not endure Meletus,—"that good man and lover of his country', for so Socrates had that day described a man renowned for his debauchery and his bad verse. Diotimus came to the rescue of the orator : "Quite so", he said, "indeed I understood all your arguments, what I could not understand was the speech and attitude of the accused."

Now the reply of Socrates to his accusers in the presence of the whole people is a wonder and a marvel to this day, so that each one of us leaned forward to listen to the outsider, if I may so describe the very worthy but somewhat voluble citizen of the New Greece, who might have grasped

THE VERDICT

what we had missed, and so supply something that would make the speeches of Socrates rational and excusable.

So it was amid an air of expectant attention, which had before been perfunctory and courteous, that Diotimus continued : " To begin with, the manner in which your prisoner replied was almost impious. I had been listening to speeches in which I recognised the true ring of oratory."

Aristophanes interrupted him and asked : " We all agree, but our friends the orators cannot ask why you say 'true ring.' I on the other hand, should be glad to know in what way the speeches were so outstanding, so that I may recognise the ring, should I be fortunate enough to hear it again ? "

" Because the speeches were polished and rhymic ", was the reply, " and the periods and balance followed so closely the examples of the last century.

" In Eos we believe that oratory ceases to be great, as such, once it breaks away from the rules and limitations that custom decrees."

Like a river in flood the Islander cleared his throat and continued : " Both of the first two speeches were delivered with a skill and in a manner which all could appreciate, and in addition with a moral force which left me, at any rate, feeling that a great ethical purpose had to be

THE VERDICT

decided by my vote, had I had that privilege. I think, too, from my experience of mankind, that the average citizen can be only keyed up to this feeling of moral worthiness by an artist who is both great and virtuous. The speech of your third prosecutor was the work of a rhapsodist, and beyond my powers of appreciation. But in reply to charges so serious—whether supported by adequate evidence or not—I had expected that the prisoner, if guilty, would appear penitent, or if innocent, would show by his manner that religion and morality were his real accusers. But this Socrates of yours from the first aggravated his audience by a flippancy both in style and argument. It even seemed to me that this man, so far from being concerned with evading his sentence or punishment, was either amusing himself at the expense of his fellow citizens, or your townsmen at his own.

"Perhaps it is because I am a stranger that I missed the strength of his case or the validity of his reply."

When he had finished speaking Diotimus looked at us each in turn, lest he should have said something unfavourable, and prepared, it may be, to recast his words, if, by any chance, he had offended against our hospitality. He was therefore visibly relieved when Neiridion supported him. Neiridion is dead, and as some of you did

THE VERDICT

not know him, I must add that he was almost a brilliant sailor, but Arginusae left him lame, and the subsequent litigation, since he was secretary to Thrasyllus, made him an old man before his time and not unnaturally a bitter opponent of democracy in all its forms.

" You are quite right in one thing, Diotimus, Socrates, whatever motive he had in replying as he did, was in no way afraid of the crowd.

" I have seen many brave men, but I have never met anyone as brave as Socrates—who has to-day been condemned to death by a mob of landsmen.

" I stood in the dock once alongside my chief, and the other Admirals of the Fleet, the victims, all of us, of professional jealousy and political passion. Socrates as President of the day, refused to put the vote, as you heard to-day when he made his Defence, but what he did not tell was how at his refusal a howl of hatred rose like a sudden squall off Delium, which made me blench, but this old man braved the whole host—but he could not prevent the murderers having their victims. Socrates despised mobs, mob leaders, and mob law, and he was not afraid to show it. What business is it of the mob, what morals a man has ; you provide censors to spy on the magistrates, and even then the laws are evaded and justice withheld—why are there no censors of morals

THE VERDICT

appointed by the State—you could then accuse a man of something definite if he provokes the censors.

"You political gentlemen value a decision obtained in the Assembly, but in the Service we have seen too many political murders to think much of the system—or the talents—which can destroy an innocent man.

"I am with Socrates—if you know that Death awaits you, it is better to laugh at him than be afraid—and that in my opinion is the reason that Socrates spoke as he did."

"No one questions his bravery", and Archion was speaking; "but why did he act like a lunatic? No man should be tired of life, and that is what Neiridion's argument amounts to. What I can't understand is this—Why should a man who was concerning himself, all day and everyday, with virtue and the like, be content to be accused of unvirtuous conduct, and raise no finger to clear his conduct or his reputation. He is accused of being cunning beyond words, and for no reason that I can find, acts like a fool and almost asks for a verdict against himself?"

"That is the crux of the whole matter", said Aristophanes. "I had intended to ponder over this by myself this evening, but since I have been beguiled here I will argue it out in public."

"Let us put it this way", I said, and I quoted

85

THE VERDICT

from the *Thesmophoriazusæ* (in my opinion the most amusing of his plays) :

> Look about in each direction,
> Make a rigid close inspection,
> Lest in any hole or corner,
> Other rogues escape detection—

and a general laugh from all except Diotimus greeted my sally.

Nothing pleased Aristophanes more than a quotation fron his own plays.

" Wait and see Neoptolemus ", he said, " before the night is over we shall hear you saying ' O dear, O dear, I cannot speak for trembling '.

" But to return to to-day. I have a feeling of personal responsibility in this prosecution, quite apart from any reference of the accused to 'a certain writer of Comedies '."

Aristophanes turned to his host holding his cup upside down, to the surprise of Diotimus, who was evidently not used to such behaviour.

" Grant me some more wine, Clinias, for I have much to say. " Having replenished his cup, he continued :

" Until *The Clouds* was acted, no one outside Sophistical circles knew very much about Socrates, and without intending it, as you all know, his influence increased very much after my play was performed."

He turned to Diotimus to explain " Bravery in Athens, we venture to think, is nothing very

THE VERDICT

unusual, but the City has cherished from earliest times her reputation for orthodoxy. My few plays have been written to safeguard this, quite as much as to stigmatise vice, or satirize the tragedians, by whom and from whom new, foreign and unwholesome opinions have crept into the community."

He was interrupted here by Aristogiton, who being young did not always think before he spoke :

" The growth of foreign ideals came from the sea, surely, rather than the tragedians " ; but he was soon taken up. " Possibly the sea, possibly the tragedians—and I will add to the list of importers of poison—bankers." It was some time before Aristogiton spoke again, for he had been the lover of Antisthenes, the banker.

The playwright continued :

" The efforts of the Best to keep religion pure, or to retain the Immortality of the Gods Immaculate, have been hampered in numberless ways. It is very difficult, for one thing, to frame an accusation of impiety, and if it had not been from his own speech in defence Socrates would have escaped with a sentence of banishment. Punishment enough, some of you will say, but it was so vital that an example should be made, and that this kind of loose thinking be stopped, that I must rejoice at the result. As to the trial itself, the accusation was definite enough, but was not

THE VERDICT

handled in my opinion in quite the right way. Let us suppose "—a very favourite expression of Aristophanes and generally masked the opening of his attack as he drawled out the "suppose"— "Let us suppose for one moment that I had the oratorical gifts of Anytus, the moral dignity of Meletus, or the rhetoric of Lycon—whom by the way I do not see at your Table, Clinias—did his rhetoric affect him ?—and that it had fallen to my lot to speak on behalf of the City and the best of her citizens. This is how I should have spoken."

As he said this both of our orators stirred uneasily on their couches, for when Aristophanes began in this strain, no one knew quite how he would end or whose self-respect would be tarnished.

" You remember that Socrates mentioned several names, whose testimony should have vindicated his character: to my mind such witness is never conclusive—for example—you Clinias are very rich, and for many nights I have drunk your wine and towards the morning at any rate we feel we understand each other. All the same I should not like to say—on my oath—that you would never steal. However well I may know you, and I know you fairly well—the testimony of Neoptolemus and Archion, say, that they saw you removing gold from the temple at night would have more weight than any witness of mine as to your moral character or, even, my repeating

THE VERDICT

that you often used to say that 'riches are an encumbrance'. I notice that you are yawning, my dear Clinias, perhaps your wine has made me tedious, so I will not say anything more about your moral character, but my point is this, that if you cannot redeem a man's reputation by mentioning the company he keeps, you can blast a man's reputation if you show that all his companions are scoundrels. Imagine me, therefore, in my best clothes, standing at the proper place and having cleared my throat, adjusted my position and my garments, speaking to my fellow citizens as follows :

" Men of Athens, do not be deceived by the tall, dignified, and handsome appearance of the prisoner, but rather pay attention to the dissolute band of ruffians who have surrounded him in the past, and like sores are festering around him to-day. You have heard from others of what things he is accused, and I know him well enough to prophesy that his defence will be that he is innocent of anything of the kind. I will not repeat these charges, but I will merely draw your attention to the characters of his friend, and associates and disciples—I warrant that you will find it sufficient.

" First, let me call one Xenophon to your mind —Xenophon, whom, by the way I do not see in the Assembly to-day. I should follow this by

THE VERDICT

a long and careful scrutiny of the Arena, and everyone would agree how wicked it was of Xenophon to be away on this day of all days; all except his friends who know as well as I do why he is away from the city.

"As I do not see him, I should go on to say, I will say, in his absence, what I am not afraid to say to his face. He is a young man of decent family but very little brains, because he will follow Socrates about open mouthed like a puppy. Perhaps it is merely a coincidence, that already in his short career he has been exiled from the city, young as he is, and has become the chosen leader of expeditions from—Sparta.

"Then, Men of Athens, do you remember Plato, the Son of Ariston—I see him standing by the side of his Master, braving the scorn of the Assembly. It had been well if he had emulated Xenophon and kept away from the scene of his crimes, for neither his charm, nor his urbanity, nor his gentleness have availed to protect him against the friendship of Socrates, from whom he has learnt the most dangerous of mental vices. —Needless to say I should not have specified what these vices were, but the very words would have conjured among the prurient minded an orgy of wickedness, and disgusted the respectable.—Thirdly I will recall to your mind, one from the dead— Alcibiades (and here I should pause to count

THE VERDICT

seven or eight under my breath), Alcibiades the stutterer, Alcibiades the profaner of mysteries ; gifted and versatile, once the hope of our City, until he too becomes the favourite companion of the prisoner, when he does his very best, and very nearly succeeds, in ruining the City and subverting the Constitution.

" His death is fresh in your memory, citizens, but the City will not cherish the memory of the inspirer of the Four hundred and the associate of Tissaphernes—and Socrates.

" One more, and I have done. You will not have forgotten Critias. This one was brought up rather than seduced into the Socratic circle. His first public effort is to write a book against democracy, his second to stir up slaves in Thessaly to revolt, his last to create in this very City a Reign of Terror, which we have not yet forgotten.

" All these, Xenophon and Plato, Alcibiades and Critias, the first two comparatively harmless, the last two actively engaged in conspiracy and intrigue against the homeland, were the favourites, the companions, the disciples of this same Socrates the Son of Sophroniscus, whom you behold in the dock to-day.

" A man who can rear such a nest of vipers among us can be no simple instructor in virtue, and whatever he may say in self-defence we must judge men by their deeds rather than their words.

91

THE VERDICT

Nor shall we this day bring like-wise to the dock those who have suffered from his teachings, but remembering that men praise that song the most which comes the newest to their ears, let us O servants of Hallanian Zeus decide that death is the punishment for such sins.

" Reserving for my peroration the words of the Poet : ' But if this seems in your eyes to be a better and more profitable thing that one man's life should be ruined without atonement, waste ye it.

" But I will call upon the Gods, that are forever, if haply Zeus may grant that deeds of requital may be wrought. Without atonement, then, should ye perish within my halls.'

" Here I should take my seat," said Aristophanes, " but you may be sure that these few simple words of mine would have been polished and adorned with any rhetorical devices that I could remember.

" I will admit that I like Socrates personally and enjoyed being in his company, but no one can deny that my speech would have been true in spirit, and that the source of many evils can be traced to this one man, who was a danger to the State, and had been better removed these fifty years. Private virtues like courage and devotion to duty cannot excuse public vices like intro-spection and prying. Socrates and his circle began by questioning themselves, they sweep up

THE VERDICT

as it were their own minds, an empty task, you will say, then they go on to scrutinise the State, and they end by peering at the Gods, and I say what I feel, the wages of such sin is death."

When the playwright had finished I turned at once to Diotimus : " You have just heard another speech, and I would ask which would have convinced you the most. Vague accusations of impiety, or detailed and definite examples of the infamous influence of the prisoner ? "

I put my question in this way on purpose, so that either the last speaker or the two orators would be annoyed, for the company was becoming unduly serious, and for another I should have been glad to have Aristophanes put upon his defence, and if he thought fit to inflict a stranger upon us, it was, as they say, his own affair.

Archion replied to the speech of Aristophanes and his deep voice rumbled across the table : " Very excellent and convincing, wasp-like as well, but it would not bring a man to his doom for impiety. If the charge had been corrupting youth or disturbing the State, your speech would have been unanswerable, but I am told that one of the charges was impiety, which is very difficult to prove as you all agree. I do not believe that Socrates by word or deed ever attempted to decry the Worship of the Goddess, but at the same time I believe him impious at heart. It is well known

THE VERDICT

that the writings of Anaxagoras were familiar to him, although towards the end I have heard he used to laugh at his reasoning, but from my own experience, I put the root of the trouble in his knowledge of that writer.

"In the third year of the War, I was back in the City when the monument that Chrisias designed was unveiled by Pericles. We cannot forget that speech, and since my young brother had fallen that year before the olive trees had put forth their young shoots, I was hard put to it not to shame you all by crying openly, when in the course of his oration Pericles uttered these words : ' We have lost the spring of the year ', and many of those around me hid their faces in their cloaks. That same night I was ordered to collect some despatches for the front, so I went to his house, or rather to the house of Aspasia.

"In his reserved way he asked a few shrewd questions, but said nothing more while he re-read his papers, until just as I was going, he looked at me and said : ' Young man, have you also left your heart upon the hillside ? ' I could not speak, but he could see well enough, for he said softly : ' We lay to rest beside this stone the memory of our young men, our high hope ', and there was a world of sorrow in his voice. Then he continued : ' You are young, and the service of the State lies before you, this will help you to

THE VERDICT

forget, but for me the time is nearly done, and hope has forsaken me. We are but puppets in the hands of Unseen Laws, but we must do as well as we can.' By this time I could speak, and what I said then I believe now : ' It is a great thing, Sir, to serve the City, and it is pleasing to the Gods.'

" ' Keep that faith as long as you can ', said Pericles, but when I was going out of the door, he added : ' but if you wish to retain it, do not read Anaxagoras.'

" As you can imagine such words were quite enough to send me to the works of this man, who came from Claxomenae, for I knew that the faith which had remained with me for two campaigns would not suffer from anything a philosopher might say. Nor did it, but I read therein opinions and doctrines which would do great harm to the State, if they should come into the hands of the mob. Now Pericles was a follower of this Anaxagoras, but he disguised it in public, but Socrates must have read the stuff and allowed it to ferment in his brain, so that he could not keep it to himself but must go everywhere talking, like a mad dog trying to bite everyone he sees. Nothing is Sacred, nothing is Holy to such men, and this way of thinking is spreading everywhere, underground and on the surface. In the last years of the War I heard the recruits talking among

THE VERDICT

themselves 'why should we die for the City' implying, if you please, that their existence mattered one way or the other. I view all this through the eyes of a soldier. When I find a man whose discipline is questioning and not absolute, for the sake of his comrades, I must stop the poison from spreading and that man has to die. We soldiers do not hold the individual as important as civilians do, we see too many good men die to take death quite as seriously. To me the virtue of Athens, and the Festivals of the Gods, and the due Sacrifice is worth more than one man's life, so that death can be the only punishment for impiety.

" No fine, no payment of money could undo the harm that Socrates and his sort have done, and it had been well, as Aristophanes said, if he had gone to the poisoner fifty years ago."

Before I could say anything to relieve the discussion, for the words and mien of Archion made it even more difficult to avoid a tragic vein, comedy returned to our banquet. The two orators who were becoming restive from their self-imposed silence, broke in upon the company, and what is more they both began together and in the same words, " We have this day saved the City."

When the laughter that this caused had subsided, Clinias spoke : " Aged poets and minstrels have a great store of old and sweet songs

96

THE VERDICT

but they find it necessary to drink a little wine to mellow them, I will have fresh wine brought in, and some grapes that you may all be refreshed."

When we had all filled our cups, I turned to Meletus : " You have been cross examined once to-day, Meletus ; would you mind if I took a hand in the game, and asked you how you had saved the City ? " " Certainly not ", he said ; " I have been enough for Socrates, so I am not afraid of anything you can say." " Well, then, in what way have you saved the City ? " " Because Socrates is as good as dead." " And you will claim that this was due to your speech ? " " I think so ", said Meletus—swelling visibly with pride. " Then if we examine the arguments in your speech, which we will not let you repeat, we shall learn how the City was saved ? " When he had agreed, I reminded him that he had accused Socrates of breeding impiety and suggesting false ideas of religion and the Gods, and when he had said " Yes ", I went on : " But tell me how the City has been saved." " Because Socrates is as good as dead ", was the reply, so I made my point at last, quite in the Socratic manner by asking him :

" But has impiety been eradicated, Meletus ?— Because, if the death of Socrates has not finally eradicated impiety, the City has not been saved."

It was quite obvious that Meletus could not

97

THE VERDICT

reply, but Anytus came to his help. With him I had more sympathy for he was quite genuine in his love for the City, and, for a professional orator, was free from those mannerisms which follow them, and actors likewise, to the grave, and even beyond if we believe what we hear. Anytus had a soft voice, whereas Meletus was strident at any time, and that night he was hoarse as well.

" No, Neoptolemus, impiety has not been stopped—I question if we can ever stop impiety, as it is as much a disease of the mind as fever is of the body. On the other hand we have to-day done a great deal to prevent impious persons spreading their poison with impunity.

" I will give an example of what I mean, when I say that we have saved the City in this way.

" When you were a child, you Neoptolemus, I mean, you were addicted to asking questions, interrogating your parents and annoying your guardians. Of this I am sure, and the present company will bear me out, since you have the same characteristics now that you are a grown man. I will go further, for I can remember you in those days, and to this day you have never ceased from doing all these things as far as they lie in your power.

" What you have evidently forgotten, but this I can vouch for, since I was often present, was, that you were well beaten by your tutor for

THE VERDICT

impertinence. For some days afterwards you ceased to be impertinent, for you had learned that certain deeds bring with them certain results, and inevitable punishment."

"That is a very weak argument", said Aristophanes.

"Very much so", I said, "and you are visiting the sins of the children upon the fathers."

"It is a weak argument, Anytus", said the playwright, "because from our knowledge of Neoptolemus, the punishment has in no way exercised that spirit of mischief, which is his only redeeming characteristic."

I repeat all this, I did not mind it at the time, although my character was being removed in handfuls, but I knew well enough that several of these present had suffered from my tongue in the past, and were also getting angry with one another.

Aristophanes continued : "You cannot eradicate impiety, punishment is of no avail, because you cannot punish people for catching fever. I quote your own example. Impiety is spread when it is displayed abroad, that is the root of my quarrel with the tragedians, and all my plays have been inspired with the idea of ridiculing such theories of life, which seem to me pernicious.

"But ridicule will kill even faster than ideas

THE VERDICT

can germinate, at least that is true of the common citizen who being morally timid is not prone to absorb new ideas very quickly, and it is the common citizen who needs protective armour the most. You will bear me out, Archion, in this, since now that you are a General, you direct your operations from your tent, while your hoplites venture in person against the swords of the enemy."

Archion did not enjoy this, for his last command had perished very rapidly owing to his plan of attack, but Aristophanes went on : " High as our civilisation may be, it is only the few, the comparative few, who can accept or resist new modes of thought. Fortunately the average man is a Conservative by nature. Nor do I think that the capacity to accept new points of view readily is desirable, since discrimination is even more rare a virtue, and new ideas are potent, like new wine is potent, to heads unaccustomed, shall I say, to such sound vintages as we are drinking to-night ", and, although he turned to Clinias and bowed, the sting lay in the words, for the wine of Clinias was as bad as his chef was good; it was a proverb in the old days.

" This fear of new ideas of religion is inherent in our blood, our whole history shows that Athens is at heart Conservative, and we have driven out these innovators, not because they are innovators and Athens is the home of civilisation, but because

THE VERDICT

iconoclastic ideas unsettle the ordinary man very much as uncooked food unsettle the digestion.

"In this company to-night, among educated men, I will admit that much to which we pay lip-service in public is beyond any credence, and even more of what is attributed to the Gods,—in my opinion erroneously—is capricious and beyond the belief of reasonable persons.

"Nevertheless, it is good for mankind generally to accept blindly that what they are taught by the priests is true in fact, and that the Gods are personally concerned in human action, and are acting accordingly. Such a belief makes men happier, and better citizens; therefore I would drive out of the City, either by banishment or death, anyone who brings disturbing thoughts before the public. During the last two years, I have noticed an increasing disposition to question not only the sublimity of the acts of the Heaven Dwellers, but the very existence of an All-Seeing Providence. This spirit of levity or impiety is what I must spend the rest of my life in fighting, whether it continues among the Tragedians, or the Sophists, or the Atheists, and these I will attack again and again so long as my ridicule remains within me, and I have breath enough to demand the death of all carriers of infection.

"I will not fear even if it leads to me being driven from the City, in foreign lands it shall

THE VERDICT

still be my boast, 'Even so I, too, fled from my country, for that I slew a man of my own kin.'"

After Aristophanes had finished speaking, something occurred which reminded me of the theatre—the impassioned accents of the chorus ceases, and some trivial character comes on to divert our attention and lighten the gloom.

My friend Eryxias, it was who broke the spell. "That speech, Aristophanes, will be well pleasing to the Gods, they will forget that you are profane, but will remember only that you were prepared to sacrifice yourself. Sacrifice is pleasing to the Gods ; they rejoice in the sacrifice of the innocent, because the value of an innocent life is great, and they rejoice in the sacrifice of the guilty because one sinner is the less. There will be rejoicing in Olympus to-night because this evil old man is condemned to death."

I think I told you that Eryxias was odd in his manner, and no one took the trouble to reply to his outburst, and the stranger from Eos, with his high pitched voice carried on the argument.

"May I speak on this subject again ? You are speaking with an advantage that I cannot claim, as Athenians, and I am not so favoured, for much which you take for granted, as it were, in the minds both of the prisoner, the audience, and his judges, seems to me beside the point.

THE VERDICT

" You will not admit, I know, that the civilisation of Eos is to be compared with your own—in many ways, apart from trade, we are deficient in our constitutional devices, we have not, for example—and here he spoke slowly and eyed us all—such an adequate—or complicated—system of ridding the State of importunate citizens. Our methods are simpler than yours. I have been listening now to so many different reasons as to why the State found it necessary to remove this man, that I can only conclude that you are more sophisticated in Athens than we are. Should similar circumstances arise in Eos—and I speak as one who has occupied positions of responsibility —we would say quite simply and none the less sincerely, this man is a nuisance to the State, and must accordingly die. Now men become nuisances to the governors, not only by intriguing with foreign governments, or by attempting to change the constitution, but in the simpler way of continuing to ask awkward questions in public.

" If you will let me continue speaking, I should like to say, what I have some hesitation in saying, partly because I am I think very much younger than the majority of these who are present, my only excuse is that I have spent the greater part of the last two years in crossing the sea and the mainland observing your differences from our island colony. In every city and every island in

103

THE VERDICT

Hellas, there seems to be a kind of sickness. You see—he added with a smile—it is not incumbent on you to travel, you have everything you require in Attica, but your humbler neighbours, not enjoying in their own right so many good things, have perforce to wander away from their homes if they are to share in what you can enjoy on your own doorstep.

" Everywhere I have been, in the Greece of the Islands, and even on the fringes of the countries of the Great King, everywhere Greek methods of habit, and Greek ways of thinking are spreading.

" But whereas I found in every City exiles, who, having travelled far and wide, were anxious to die in their own cities. When they departed for their homes, they left behind them the songs of Greece and the knowledge of our Holy religion, but carried back with them an attitude towards life which was foreign to Greek civilisation, and which has already produced a crumbling effect, if I may use the expression, in our Hellenic ideals.

" It has always seemed to me that all we value so highly in our method of life is only suitable for insular kingdoms, and a limited world. For example, our fathers looked upon the Great King almost as a monster of mythology, a dim but maleficient progidy, we know him now to be a man like ourselves, maleficient perhaps, but limited, and with a perverted passion for women.

THE VERDICT

As the habitable world has grown smaller, and as War has increased our knowledge of geography, we learn that we are no longer self-sufficient, and the habits of even barbarians become of academic interest.

" This has induced throughout Hellas (I am speaking of what I have seen) a sort of questioning wonder, if, if anything we have wrought by ourselves, free from barbarian influence, is so very valuable after all. Once having admitted that, since good can come, from Macedon, shall I say, everything that we previously considered Holy from habit, has become open to enquiry.

" This prevalent habit of questioning is by no means confined to your City—that I can assure you from my own experience—nor are yours the only citizens who are faced with the problem of a Socrates.

" And after all, you Athenians are the last who should prohibit such things, for unless my memory is wrong you have not been slow in the past to bring a critical enquiry to bear upon the authority, or the usefulness, or the strength of your neighbours. If you do not countenance this spirit of enquiry within your own circle as yet, the time will soon come when it will be everywhere, and no longer amenable to either poisoner or banishment. Therefore I say that your trial was unnecessarily long, and—unless it gave pleasure to the populace

THE VERDICT

thereby—a waste of time, and I think your prisoner, your Socrates, was ahead of his time, as we say, and uncannily correct, when he prophesied that future generations would say that you had not acted wisely in this matter."

" Prisoners ", interrupted Aristophanes, " at least prisoners condemned to death, always appeal to posterity, they have no other tribunal who can help them. If it lay in my power to stem the inroads of barbarism, which you, Diotimus, have so glibly told us is knocking at our doors, I would still slay and slay, in order that our antient virtue be kept—and the glory of Hellas remain incorruptible."

But when Aristophanes gets vindictive, wine has the effect of making him surly as well as rude, instead of being amusing and rude, so Clinias took up the argument by saying :

" We have all been very interested in your point of view, Diotimus, but after all, you have travelled, looking rather for the diseases of Greece, if you will permit me to say so, than the endurance of our civilisation.

" All the same what you have said reminded me very much of another of the speeches of Pericles. Most of us here present can remember him, his distant manner, his beauty, both of mind, and figure and voice.

" By the way, Archion referred to Pericles, and

THE VERDICT

the almost notorious impiety of the lady of his choice—but we must remember that we no longer live in times of security.

" When Pericles was our controller, Athens was safe and strong enough to stomach a play called The Acharnians, such strong meat to-day would bring the author, like Socrates, to death. So that arguments as to what was permissible then, are no longer applicable to conditions as we know them now. Old established states, when prosperous, can easily withstand criticism from within, but after disasters in the field, or diplomacy, it is natural for the bulk of the citizens to depend on such virtues as are considered to be free from the threat of decay; and to distrust, almost hysterically, any of these new fangled ideas, which are so prevalent to-day. Our City politically is uncertain of herself—almost if you will forgive the apparent impiety—like a Goddess, who is accused before High Heaven of having a liaison with the Thunderer, and does not know whether she can laugh it away as of no moment, or whether she must proclaim it on the housetops as a serious affair.

" The first year of the War, Pericles made one of these speeches which will be remembered long after any of us here have joined the Immortals, and something he then said has some bearing on what Diotimus has said.

THE VERDICT

"Diotimus spoke of that spirit of inquisitiveness or mental alertness which was to corrode away the atmosphere of Greece in general.

"Pericles thought otherwise—and this is what he said, speaking in our City:

"'This liberty which we enjoy is the administration of the State, we use also with one another in our daily course of life, neither quarrelling with our neighbour for following his own humour, nor casting on him censorious looks, which, though they be no punishment, yet they grieve.'

"I like to think that the whole speech was an everlasting memorial to all that we value, in that it faithfully portrayed our life, and, what is more, our attitude to life. I thought it true then, but if Diotimus is correct—and we must remember that the stranger within our gates often sees that is hidden, or perhaps unpleasant—this ideal of ours has either never existed or has carried within itself the seeds of decay.

"To be quite candid the pleasant, unpleasant truth teller has always been licensed in this City—we are content to banish our citizens just as soon for a surplus of virtue as a surplus of vice—Aristides is a case in point—for in every way we value moderation. To my mind citizens who are too good are just as much an interference or blot upon our corporate body as citizens who are too inquisitive, or too wicked.

THE VERDICT

"Now Eryxias is just as much a nuisance as Socrates, tho' in a different way—he is for ever arguing about the services of the Goddess, and why some things are done, and others are left undone. To my mind he is seditious, and causes dissension among the pious, or those other little-minded persons who believe that the Gods can be interested in the details of existence. He only escapes punishment because he is on the side of authority.

"Let us get back to Socrates—he was never to my mind too good, he was exceedingly amusing and well-mannered—and undertook every duty that came his way—a little officious perhaps, but that is permitted to old men, as we have a misguided idea that the old are necessarily wise. But impious, he never was, and if Eryxias will not interrupt me or bring down curses upon me, I will say that a great deal of nonsense is talked about piety and impiety, religion and irreligion which Socrates to do him justice would never countenance for one moment.

"The Athenians pay lip-service to the worship of the Gods in general, and to our patron, the Goddess Athene in particular. We are accustomed to receive from the priests—and the Sacred College—if you will allow me to coin such an expression—certain—or should I say uncertain—facts, theories or conjectures, or what is true of the Immortals. We are civilised enough in spite

THE VERDICT

of anything that Diotimus has seen, to behave ourselves seemly at the festivals—some of us may even appear devout—but you my friends know perfectly well that the well-educated among us do not believe in the greater part of the official creed. On the other hand the religion of the State, we believe, and believe devoutly, is a great binder-together, so that when the democracy at large is bidden to accept the Athene-legend and her mystical benevolence, we can join them so far in believing that an Immortal power is guiding our destinies, but whereas they call this power Athene and visualise a very gracious Lady, we would call it The Soul of Athens.

" And those of us who are well-educated would certainly band ourselves together with those who are ignorant against any man whose existence or morality was a threat to the well-being of the City, or whose influence was foreign or antagonistic to all that the name of Athens conjures to each one of us. Such a man would certainly be poisoned—although again a certain hypocrisy—inherent in all men where affairs of the conscience are concerned—would compel us to charge and condemn him on some other charge—such as impiety for instance.

" To my mind the real driving force behind the prosecution we are considering was political and not religious, the real danger to our State is not

THE VERDICT

that it may be stifled by atheists, but that it should be corrupted by sinister social interests.

"Now Socrates admitted to being a gadfly, flying about and asking questions. We have no quarrel with a man for following his own humour, nor can the State make his particular habit a capital offence, notwithstanding that, for reasons that I will come to later, he is charged with corruption and impiety.

"There is always a certain amount of corruption of youth—after all youth was created to be corrupted, as Diotimus has said, otherwise we should have no men, or comedies either—but in the accusation Socrates was not associated with those Mysteries which are beginning to claim so many votaries among the citizens, and to my mind are definitely corrupt and pernicious and demoralising and foreign to Hellas. I have been a companion of Socrates for many years, and he is one of the last men I should call impious, for he was definitely a genuine believer in the Divine, but equally definitely not, in the Gods as they generally represented to us—on the other hand his sense of duty, which grew more highly developed as he grew older compelled him to try and increase the number of those that believed or could believe on the same lines as himself.

"This is what he said himself to-day speaking from the Dock: 'For I do nothing but go about

THE VERDICT

persuading you all, young and old alike, not to take thought for your persons or properties, but first and chiefly to take care about the greatest improvement of the Soul.' It is in no way contrary to the Hellenic spirit to create a school or colony of sympathisers, nevertheless it has that which has brought Socrates to his death to-day.

"As I get older, wiser, who knows, I find an increasing amusement in tracing the motives of human action, and in discovering what a large number of political causes spring from motives which are purely mercenary. If you have agreed with me that Socrates was not a corrupter of youth, or an impious person, you will have also agreed with me that he was not doing anything foreign to our ideals in proselytising or spreading his doctrines abroad in lectures or conversations or the like. But Socrates was the first man I ever heard of who discussed wisdom or virtue without charging fees, and if you are still patient I will explain why I believe that Socrates has been sent to his death. You would think I was mad if I suggested that our old friend Eryxias here could be moved by mercenary ideas in any shape or form, and yet it seems to me that he has the mind of a tradesman, or a banker, or a money changer. Have I your permission to assume the mien of Socrates himself and ask him a few questions ? "

THE VERDICT

In spite of the length of Clinias' arguments, we were all listening intently, for Clinias had a delightful voice which was capable of many delicate shades of expression, and besides anything he said was out of the ordinary, and he had too a way of using his hands to amplify his asides which fascinated me, and this tended to keep his audience awake and alert. You may be sure that Eryxias brightened up considerably at being asked to take a part in the argument, for like most of us he was quite willing to express his opinions on the events of the day, possibly also with just as much right, so he cleared his throat, a habit he had acquired from his clerical friends, and replied :

" Certainly, Clinias, so long as you will say nothing against the Services of the Gods."

" Well, Eryxias, every year in Athens, we hold a service do we not, in which a procession of suitably clothed persons walk before the Statue of the Goddess ? "

" That is quite true."

" And it is the custom also, for the pious to give of their means that the worship of Athene may be suitably conducted ? "

" Certainly."

" And you know likewise that such offerings are weighed up and the amount recorded, at the end of the Festival ? "

THE VERDICT

" Yes ", said Eryxias, and " I myself have been for some years past one of these who do these things."

" That is better still," said Clinias, " for you can tell us from your own knowledge."

" I know," said Eryxias, " but I cannot tell you, for these things are secret, and I have sworn not to divulge them except to properly authorised persons."

" I would not ask you the exact amount ", Clinias continued, " but you can answer me this—was not the collection this year less than last year's ? "

" That is correct, Clinias, I can answer you that without breaking my oath—the collection was less."

" Can you answer me this—was not the collection of last year, less in the same way than that of the previous year ? "

" There were very good reasons ", said Eryxias. " I am sure there were, there are always good reasons ", said our host, and went on : " Though it is doubtful if we should agree as to what these reasons were, but I will not go into that, instead I will ask you one more question :

" Is it not true that for the last six years the annual contribution of the pious at the Annual Festivals has been decreasing ? "

After a good deal of pressure Clinias got his

THE VERDICT

answer that the money received was decreasing as had been suggested.

" That is sufficient for me ", said Clinias. "Now let us see whom Socrates has succeeded in antagonising in the last ten years, not merely by being himself and asking awkward questions in public—that would apply to Neoptolemus—and no one would think him worthy of death, you will find that they are those persons whose livelihood or properties were jeopardised by the spread of the Socratic wisdom or creed.

" Among the first were those rich men who had good-looking and intelligent sons. For some reason or other, whether because they had more spare time or were better educated, such youths were chiefly to be found in the company of Socrates; and it was sufficiently remarkable that his disciples were notoriously indifferent to money. I have noticed that rich fathers take it especially hard when their sons become indifferent to money, it implies that something is lacking, either in the acquisitions of the Sires, or the acquisitiveness of the Sons, in either case it seems to hurt, at any rate here was a nucleus for those who had reason to hate Socrates.

" The next class who were offended at him were the Sophists, which for the purpose of my theory includes all the lawyers, the orators, the politicians, and the actors.

THE VERDICT

"Sophists—splendid foreigners who flit like meteors across our City, leaving only tails (which are found to be built up of the flimsiest materials) behind them.

"'Who go round the cities'—as the accused said, to-day—how he hated these—ultra-professional-good-fellows! These were his enemies, because their special knowledge was their livelihood, acquired by spending money in fees to the professors, whereas Socrates taught that virtue or skill could not be bought by money alone, and furthermore that he would sell the same for nothing into the bargain. You will admit that it must be annoying, to say the least, for a professional man to be told that what had cost him a great deal was worth nothing and could be acquired for nothing.

"Thirdly, Socrates had antagonised those whose livelihood depended on the religion of our Lady. His teaching, as far as I could understand it, was to learn how to acquire virtue, rather than purchase it, and as his influence and his circle became wider and wider, so the formalities of worship, and the concomitant offerings grew less and less (Eryxias has confessed that the sums received from the faithful has been decreasing for the last six years), and during that time, the influence of Socrates, whether direct or indirect, has been growing considerably, very much more than many of you here realise.

THE VERDICT

" The priests were against Socrates, not because he made amusing remarks about the priesthood, for you Aristophanes have not refrained from doing that, but whereas all your influence is to drive people into the temples—and the theatres —the influence of Socrates was to drive people into themselves. Thus then, all these influential bodies of persons could see in the continued existence of Socrates, a threat against their wealth or livelihood.

" They decide, then, to accuse him of something—and when I say 'they decide', I do not mean that they met in conclave for that purpose, but that events forced them to take some action, and that this compulsion grew and grew until it reached the finality we have witnessed to-day.

" So, willy nilly, Socrates has to be accused of something—it is called impiety, if you like—" said Clinias, shrugging his shoulders, " a pretty general kind of accusation, which may mean anything or nothing, but carries with it to our citizens an atmosphere of something almost unbearable and disgraceful.

" Impiety offends the ordinary citizen, it is the immoderate extravagant kind of thing which offends his taste, and his peace of mind, and the strength of custom.

" The actual accusers themselves are chosen

THE VERDICT

with a consideration both of their piety and their sophistical skill, and, in spite of their better judgment, a further charge of corrupting youth is added to their brief by the enemies of Socrates.

" The accused does not rely for his defence on his undoubted virtues, but almost laughs at the charge, and, with a touch of genius, offers in exchange for his life, with a sense of irony which is worthy of Euripides at his best, an exceedingly small sum of money.

" That is how it seems to me, my dear friends— and I will confess I enjoyed the trial from the beginning to the end. I even recorded my vote, but I shall not tell you how I did vote. Whatever else that old man had met and suffered in his long life, he was not afraid of Death, and that is the memory I shall hope to have with me, when my time comes to die."

By the time that Clinias had finished speaking, the wine on the table had been drunk, and none of us had dared to interrupt our host, who was so obviously enjoying his own argument, so Aristophanes began immediately : " You must be thirsty Clinias, and I would ask you to fill your cup, but that your friends have drunk everything they can find." This had the effect of producing what we had all been seeking, and what pleased Aristophanes the more, making Clinias feel

118

THE VERDICT

abashed, so in a good temper, so far as he could be in a good temper, Aristophanes continued :

" The worst of you rich men is that you become distorted, and view everything in relation to wealth, —I thank the Gods, if so educated a company can permit such language—I thank the Gods, that wealth does not control either my opinions, my religion or my plays. I suppose you will even find a deep mercenary motive in all my master-pieces. You are an amusing fellow, Clinias, far more amusing than I am. You may have convinced Diotimus that Socrates was done to death by the devices of rich men like yourself— and without your sense of humour you would never have convinced Aristogiton that your theories are correct, but by the Robe of Athene, you have very nearly convinced me. Had I had sufficient of your wine, you might really have done so."

Neiridion interrupted him : " Is this comedy finished, if comedy is the correct term ?

" You have each of you showed many good reasons why Socrates must die. Let me ask you this : ' Is it not likely that even now you will fail in your hopes—what is to prevent Socrates with the aid of his friends from breaking prison, as we say, and, embarking on the high seas, sail like another Helen to light another Troy ? ' "

119

THE VERDICT

Such a simile from the stern sailor made it evident to me that the wine of Clinias was more potent than we had imagined, and I looked round the table to see flushed faces everywhere save for Meletus and Diotimus, and their heads were buried in their arms. Three only, besides myself, of that company were in a position to continue the discussion, Archion the soldier, Eryxias the madman, and Aristogiton the most youthful of us all.

It was Aristogiton who continued, his voice was still fresh, and it was evident that he had not been drinking much, for there was scorn in his voice, and it is difficult to be scornful when drunk.

" Have no fear ", I heard him say, " have no fear that Socrates will try to escape." Then as he noticed that only Archion and I were listening he turned to us : " You none of you knew that I attended the lectures of Socrates, and I kept silent, to-night, only because I feared to deny him before you all. Nor can you imagine how I have chafed because I could not speak up for him against his enemies. Only six weeks ago, or at any rate before any of us knew that the accusation had been made, he spoke to us on our duty to the State. How we must never avoid the duties to the State which the Gods laid upon us—for he said duty is an officious kind of taskmaster, which cannot be bribed, as an official of the State can be bribed, but can only be accepted, driven away, or

120

THE VERDICT

drugged. When I remember that, I cannot believe that Socrates will avoid any burden that comes his way. At the same time, he told us that sometimes the burden of duty was divided, in that the duty which a man owed to the State was hostile and in conflict with other duties, and he read to us the story of Antigone, pointing out that she, a king's daughter, was torn between two duties, her duty to her King, and her duty to her brother's memory."

It might almost have been of himself that he spoke that day as he ended with these words : .

" When such things befall us, it will not avail us to revile Fate and say ' Woe is me ' ; let us rather go forward doing such things as are most seemly and according to the virtue that is within us. Rather let us say when the agony has been shouldered, and, it may be, that death himself has to be faced, speaking to our comrades and friends to encourage them likewise ; 'Live on thou —but know that my soul long since has died,' Socrates was the first of the martyrs to the domination of the State and the crushing of individual choice, he will not be the last. The combat between the Soul and the State is the battle ground of the future."

These words interested me very much, for the lectures of Socrates had not been common property as we say, but were kept by his disciples, almost like a mystery, so I asked the diffident youth what

THE VERDICT

Socrates had really said about the Gods, since now there could be no harm done to his Master, and I wondered if after all there might not be some truth in all this chatter about impiety. As you can imagine, impiety did not effect me very much, and I hoped it would stimulate Eryxias.

"I cannot say what impiety can be", he replied; "if Socrates was impious, I will only tell you what I have heard him say. The Gods, or The Good, may be compared to a stream of water flowing down a hill side. Such a stream seems to us to follow its own opinion as to how or where it should go, so long as it conforms to the rule of nature, which for water, is that it should move to the sea. It is the custom of the priests, Socrates said, to claim that both the channel of the stream and the very water itself are both their province and their property. They permit the worshippers at the temple to take away the water, which they aver is sacred, into their own homes, stipulating only the shape of the bottles in which the water shall be taken away—incidentally they are accustomed to sell the precise kind of bottle, without which they claim that the water will lose its virtue. Then Socrates would explain to us that the bottle in which the water was retained was immaterial—but that it was unreasonable to put such sacred water into bottles which had held wine or other liquids, until they had been well

THE VERDICT

cleaned, but what we should chiefly venerate was the water itself.

"Then he added, it was wisest, both for the recipient and indeed for the water's sake, to partake of this water by drinking it. I can hear him speaking now, in his dry way. 'But it is better to partake of such water unto oneself rather than carrying it away in a bottle, for no water is eternal unless it is drunk.'"

And with these words his memories overcame him, and Aristogiton wept.

I could not endure to witness his tears, so I arose and with me came Eryxias and Archion, leaving behind us the boy in tears and the rest of the company asleep.

THE CITY OF GOD

THE CITY OF GOD

But where thine infinite sky spreadeth for the Soul to take for flight, a stainless white radiance reigneth ! wherein is neither day nor night, nor form nor colour, nor ever any word.

Gitanyati. TAGORE.

After celebrating a marriage, he went to the City which he founded for himself, and was established in the house of ZEUS.

Odyssey, VI, 209.

CHARACTERS

Euphorbion — Plato's copyist

Plato — —

Simonides : a Slave Plato's house steward

Attis : a Slave — The adviser of Dion

Neoptolemus A rich Athenian

Hamilcar — — A Carthaginian merchant

Jason — — A Tutor

THE CITY OF GOD

In the Autumn of that same year that the Macedonians sent hostages to Thebes, and the Greeks sent envoys to Susa, I learnt from my Master that he had decided to leave the City for Syracuse. I was not unprepared for this, since I had been listening for many nights to the arguments of the messengers from Dion, and although it did not concern me directly, I had been hoping to the end that Plato would remain in Athens. I could not understand how anyone, let alone Plato, could tear himself away from the scent of the Sea off the Piræus, the sunrise glorifying the Acropolis, and the shadow of the spear of the Goddess lengthening as the day waned. The seventeen years that I could remember had all been hallowed by these things, for although I was born, or so they said, in Sparta, I could remember nothing of the wall-less city.

But once the decision was made, it fell to me to finish as soon as I could copying out such rolls as my Master required in his new venture.

The evenings in Attica that autumn were cold, so that each night I lighted a fire in the library, and when my hand grew too cramped to write any

THE CITY OF GOD

more, I used to sit and watch the logs burning. This night, I remember, I sat so long that I had to light a lamp the room had grown so dark, and when I had settled down to work again, I re-read the passage I had just completed. "Wherefore God, the orderer of all, in his tender care, seeing the world was in great straits, and fearing that all might be dissolved in the storm and disappear in Infinite Chaos, again seated himself at the helm."

Very much the position of my Master, I thought, recollecting what the Sicilians had said the state of Syracuse would be unless Plato came over to help them, and I read on, "and bringing back the elements which had fallen into dissolution and disorder to the motion which had prevailed under his former dispensation, he set them in order and restored them, and made the world imperishable and immortal." So apposite a quotation for the work in view seemed like a propitious omen, I had not noticed it when copying, as the eye and hand are too busy doing their work for the mind to follow the process of thought, at least that is my experience, but coming to it fresh, as it were, I could not help wondering if my Master would find it so easy to administer a state in real life as to lay down rules for the guidance of rulers in theory, from his study.

I was so absorbed in thinking of this that I did not hear the curtain thrust aside, nor know that

THE CITY OF GOD

Plato himself was behind my chair till I heard him say.

" ' Imperishable and Immortal ', that is a good place for anyone to stop their work. Let us come together, Euphorbion, and see how many places Simonides has laid for supper."

I put out the lamp and as he took my arm for the short distance that separated the Library from the House, the bats flew between the columns as we walked up the stone path.

You must know that since the Academe had been opened, strangers from the whole world came to talk with my Master, and nothing delighted him more than those hours spent with fresh and alert minds when supper was over and the worries of the day had been smoothed away. For myself I delighted to hear of fresh cities and new worlds, so long as I could remain in Athens, but my Master's mind was more nimble than mine, and for the time being he would become a citizen of each new city and share in the enjoyment of an exile's memory ; perhaps, because I was an exile myself, I could enjoy their stories without emotion, but I confess I dreaded the thoughts of the evenings in store without Plato and intelligent strangers.

I had been convinced in my own mind that Plato had decided to go, for I had noticed that since the Ambassadors from Sicily had come and had begun to argue with him that he should

THE CITY OF GOD

leave Athens, a kind of mental excitement seized him. He had become more restive, and could not settle down to the routine of his lectures, but would pore over his map. His habit of conversation at dinner too was changed, instead of following some special argument like a bloodhound on the trail, he would break off the hunt and talk of Sicily. He admitted this himself and said with a laugh : " I am become like that watchman in *Antigone,*

> Winding thus about
> I hastened, but I could not speed, and so
> Made a long journey of a little way."

When we reached the hall, the house was a blaze of light, and he called out :

" Simonides, is this the feast of lamps in Sais ?
—For whom is all this light ? "

Simonides was now an old man ; he had been steward since Ariston had died, and like so many slaves born into the household he had become one of the family, and therefore familiar, insufferably familiar I often thought.

He was not in the best of tempers that night and came in grumbling : " The lamps are lit because it is your dinner hour, and no less than four hungry strangers are hanging about till you are good enough to come in. A good dinner spoilt as usual. It might be a feast of Theseus, barley meal and bread, for all you care."

132

THE CITY OF GOD

All my Master said was : " Then my bath will have to be short. Go, Euphorbion, and find out who has come. Attis and Neoptolemus I expected, but who the others are, I don't know. Say to them such things as will soothe them, and put them round the table so that I sit between the strangers." Thereupon I went into the dining-room, to find both Attis and Neoptolemus. Attis was a big stout man, who was from his own account the favourite slave of Dion, but although he did not say so in as many words, quite as certainly the brain and counsellor as well. Neoptolemus was big, too, but much fatter. He was a very rich Athenian who knew everybody worth knowing and many others as well. Besides these two, were others, strangers to me, who had come with Attis. One a short dark man in highly coloured clothes, which reminded me somehow of the Phrygians, or the sailor merchants from Tyre, his name was Hamilcar and Drepana his city, wherever that might be. I learnt he was a trader in carpets and armour. The last was a Macedonian, Jason by name, who was the guardian of one of the young princes from the North residing as a hostage in Thebes. It was obvious that he thought himself important, but it was in no way my duty to disillusion him.

I had barely time to sort them out and put them round the table when Plato returned, and having

THE CITY OF GOD

spoken to reach in turn, saying such things as would put the most shy of strangers at their ease, we began to eat.

For some reason or other Simonides considered the evening of importance as he had roasted a kid to supplement our usual meal of bread, butter and honey, cheese and a salad, figs and grapes.

During the first part of the meal little was said, this also was usual when Plato was tired ; he used to say that sleep and death might be twin brethren, but silence and digestion likewise went hand in hand.

Neoptolemus started the conversation, with his mouth full of kid, I remember, by turning to the head of the table saying : " What's this I hear of your leaving the City again, Plato ? From the number of miserable boys I see every morning trudging into your Academe, I should have thought things had been going well with you ? "

" What you have heard is true ", was the reply ; " but I am not going away because my lecture-rooms are full or empty."

" Bigger fees somewhere else, I suppose ? " said the Athenian.

Simonides came into the room then with the wine, so Neoptolemus turned to him : " What a tyrant you are, Simonides. You are driving your Master from home because you won't give him enough wine."

THE CITY OF GOD

" Tyrant ! ", said Simonides, " I'm not such a tyrant as some I know. And you, Neoptolemus, would be none the worse for a little less wine. But its no good blaming me if he goes. I've told him often enough if he goes back to those heathen, they'll only sell him for a slave again."

" Slavery is another experience, no more and no less ", was my Master's reply. " We must not complain or blame either Gods or men for putting us in the way of further experience."

" Pelion and Ossa ! " ejaculated Neoptolemus, who for once seemed at a loss for a word. " Don't tell me that you are rash enough to go back to Sicily ? "

" I am, indeed, Neoptolemus. But take comfort to thy soul, as I am to follow in the footsteps of Ulysses, I have made my peace with Poseidon saying these words :

" ' Reverend even in the eyes of the Immortal Gods is that man who comes as a wanderer, even as I have now come to thy stream and to thy knees, after many toils.'

" But, lest some one is listening who may tell tales in Olympus, I will ask Attis if I have been light-hearted about the matter, or if, indeed, I have decided to go without much persuasion."

Attis laughed at this : " No by Dagon you have not."

135

THE CITY OF GOD

" I don't know him ", said Neoptolemus, shrugging his shoulders.

" Know whom ? " asked Attis, a little nettled by his manner, and it was natural enough.

" This Dagon person."

Here the gentleman from Drepana joined in. His accent was barbaric enough to put Neoptolemus in a good temper at once. " Dagon is a great God in Syracuse ", and he said it as if he was explaining his nurse to a small boy.

" Of course, of course ", he replied ; and he bowed smiling to the stranger. " I remember him perfectly now you remind me. Stupid of me, wasn't it ? One of the Scaly Gods, a little— undignified—shall I say, to our ideas, but graceful enough, I am sure in his own element."

To prevent anything worse being said Plato turned to Attis : " I think you had better explain, otherwise Neoptolemus will tell everyone that I have been driven away for trying to introduce new Gods into the City."

Attis looked round at us all before replying, and beneath his shaggy eyebrows I could see a twinkle in his eyes : " New Gods are never amiss in this city, are they Plato ? but I will free you from the accusation. I will admit also for the benefit of those who tell tales, in Olympus, that I had great difficulty in persuading you, and if Poseidon must blame anyone he must blame me."

136

THE CITY OF GOD

Somehow Attis annoyed the rich Athenian.

" What a comfort for Poseidon ", he remarked. " Your position in the world must be good enough if you can patronise the Gods, and what is the harder task, I venture to think—can persuade Plato to leave Athens."

But Attis was only the more amused from his reply : " I am but a slave in the household of Dion ", he said.

" Dion ? ", queried Neoptolemus. " Dion—I must confess my ignorance—is he a God, too ? "

" Dion is not exactly a God, but he is powerful enough in his own place. You see this purple stripe on my arm "—so saying he pointed to the broad purple band which fringed his sleeves— " that is sufficient to give me entrance into any palace in Sicily—not always a welcome perhaps ", and his eyes twinkled again ; " but I will go so far as to say that my wishes are generally effective wherever I go—in Sicily."

" But who is Dion ? " was all that he got in reply.

" If you will cross the sea, Athenian, you will not ask that question after one night on the island. Sicily is ruled by Syracuse, and Syracuse obeys Dionysius, Dionysius listens to the voice of Dion."

" Yes ", said Neoptolemus, " and Dion listens to Attis, I suppose ? "

137

THE CITY OF GOD

All that Attis said, in spite of the rude manner of his neighbour was : " I have known him take my advice."

Hamilcar leant forward to speak : " Let me explain to you the state of politics in the Island, that you may understand better.

" Some of your cities on the mainland are content with a tyrant, with chains of adamant and the spears of a bodyguard. Our rulers in Sicily are content to rule, behind the scenes as it were. My friend here is one of those, fortunate and rare amongst men, who rules a tyrant, and what is still rarer, does not boast it abroad. Not so long ago Dionysius died, and tho' the word of Dion can conjure up armies and ships, and tho' he is one of the richest men in the world, yet he will not make himself master but is content to serve the son of his benefactor, his own nephew. He is a marvel among men, is this Dion, for he has great dreams, and his ambition—at least as far as I can understand it—is that tyranny shall be no more, and the new tyrant shall be controlled.

" He has a greater quality than any I have mentioned yet, he is, and has for a long time been a disciple of Plato, the son of Ariston," and Hamilcar finished his statement with a courteous bow to his host.

" Very delightfully put ", said Neoptolemus ; " but you must excuse my Athenian obtuseness

138

THE CITY OF GOD

when I see no reason in all this for my good friend Plato the son of Ariston in leaving Athens."

It was Plato's turn to smile as he said :

" Because I too am a disciple of a better man than myself."

" No, I won't have that ", said Neoptolemus ; " you remember what Aristophanes said."

" That man he's following is a poor blind man." But Plato refused to be turned aside.

" Having been a slave once, I have the advantage of some of you, because I can give free play to my own humour. These ten years I have been lecturing on the science of ruling the mind of the ruler—it is a science—and explaining as far as I could how the philosopher king must learn his business.

" Surely my duty is plain. There in Sicily, not so very far away after all, is a young boy whose father after a career of refined blood thirst—I speak for a moment as a democrat—has gone to the land where tyranny at least is disembodied. If this lad has ability he may succeed in becoming a tyrant no better (or no worse if you like) than his father—but the boy has something more than ability to help him, he enjoys the friendship of Dion, who was his father's right hand, and—my friend.

" Dion is no lover of tyranny—although after all, much may be said for such a method of

139

THE CITY OF GOD

government—in Sicily, but Dion has seen enough of the world of politics to know that Democracy is sometimes far more unpleasant for Democrats than a tyranny—for that at the least can be tempered by assassination—and you can only temper Democracy with pestilence. Quite naturally my friend desires that this boy should be trained in the art of Government, and although for many years my friendship with Dion has been a source of joy—to me at any rate—unfortunately he knows that I have been in the habit of lecturing on the more desirable methods of educating our rulers; you know this well enough, Euphorbion, as you have been copying out my books for his benefit.

" I talked about a sense of humour. Well here, Neoptolemus, is the application. You know how foolish a doctor becomes when he is overtaken by illness, it seems to us laymen—if I may coin such an expression—a contradiction in ideas that a physician of our bodies should be unwilling or unable to cure himself.

" How foolish therefore should I seem, having taken pains to explain during so many happy years, what valuable medicine for sick kings I kept in my pocket and then to refuse my help to a tyrant who was convalescent.

" Then, too, I have never escaped from almost a passion for Sicily itself, and in my previous

THE CITY OF GOD

journeyings in and about that island I have always been conscious that I was but following in the footsteps of Ulysses, whom, you will all admit was at any rate an intelligent person."

All this time Simonides had not left the room and he surprised us with a strident laugh :

" Ha, ha ! Yes ! But if I remember aright one Circe has something to say to lovely strangers.

" Don't forget, Plato, that she caught you once and turned you into a slave. Take care she doesn't capture you again and convert you into something strange a second time."

Plato continued : " I do not know why you consider a slave such a dreadful beast, Simonides, after all you are happy enough. But you are like everyone else who leads a sheltered life, you are afraid of poverty—and it is the fear of poverty that freezes the soul. It is nicer perhaps to own one's own house, and therein do what one wishes rather than what some-one else wishes, but after all slavery is no worse than marrying a wife, and in other respects we have, none of us, very much choice in what we do in this life, at any rate as we grow old. For instance, at my age I have to live the kind of life to which my body has become accustomed, a little food, less wine and a quantity of lectures. You, Neoptolemus, consume more food, a good deal more wine, and no lectures at all, except my present speech for which I apologise.

141

THE CITY OF GOD

Freedom of mind is by no means inconsistent with slavery, and as far as I am concerned I am fairly safe from further bondage as my body will no longer command a fair price in the slave market."

As he finished speaking the merchant from Drepana, although he could not appreciate the asides of the soliloquy of my Master, punctuated as it was with a smile or a mere flick of his fingers to apply his aphorisms, felt it incumbent upon him to add something of his native wood notes wild—so he said : " Sicily, beautiful island—beautiful slave market ! " to lean back quite satisfied that he had benefited the conversation.

Attis, not the least of the company to enjoy such things and, if I may say so, internally twinkling, continued : " I know the island as well as most men, Plato, but never before have I heard it connected with the Odyssey. That there are dangers for navigators round Sicily, no one will deny, but if what you say is true, there are more succulent dangers than Circe or even Charybdis. What would Calypso say, or rather for how much would she release you, O friend of Dion, my Master, if she should find you on her territory ? "

" Rather than these things should happen, I would that I might meet with white armed Nausicaa ", said Plato.

THE CITY OF GOD

" But I have finished my traffic with such merchants by now, Attis. I am much more frightened of a bagful of winds. Seriously—and he smiled round the table to add force to his words —Sicily has become for me the scene of the journeys of Ulysses since I met Hannibal, a slave who worked beside me when I too bore the yoke.

" Hannibal was a scribe, not so good a one as you, Euphorbion, but nevertheless interesting as he had made himself an authority on the poet, and had spent many years in connecting the adventures of Ulysses with various parts of Sicily. He certainly convinced me then that the geography of the Odyssey was none other than your island. I have often noticed by the way that the most searching and appreciative criticism of the works of the poets come from those who are aliens.

" But if you want to talk of Homer, you must ask Euphorbion, for he is an authority on all his work. "

All I could say to this was to ask another question :

" If Sicily is the scene of the wanderings, where in that island may this spot be found ? ", and I recited the description of the garden of Alcinous :

Therein grew trees, tall and luxuriant, pears and pomegranates and apple trees, with their bright fruit, and sweet figs and luxuriant vines. Of these the fruit perishes not, nor fails in winter or in summer, but lasts throughout the year, and ever does the west wind, as

143

THE CITY OF GOD

it blows, quicken the life of some fruits, and ripen others,
pear upon pear waxes ripe, apple upon apple, cluster
upon cluster, and fig upon fig.
There too is the fruitful vineyard planted.

" That, Euphorbion, is true of all Sicily—you,
Attis, will bear me out. I know no land more
lovely—anywhere, and he paused for a moment
to add—or more cruel. The mountains in Sicily
cease to be temperate, and although they are
covered with snow at the proper time, bear within
them the fire of their father Poseidon ; but
mountainous and snow clad, and fierce tho' they
be, they are still beautiful. Moreover, in the most
unexpected places, at the head of ravines, which
are dotted with trees and ravished with water,
and on the top of the most difficult cliffs, appear
delightful small temples to new and strange gods
of those mountains, Who knows but in that magic
isle I might yet find the footsteps of Pan or hear
the lyre of Apollo.

" Be present with us all, favourable omens" ;
so saying he filled his cup and poured out libations
in due silence.

" Sicily is the land of Poseidon ", he continued ;
" with such a sire you cannot expect the animals
that breed there to be tame, nor are they—
even— " and he paused for a moment and then
continued " even the poets are full-blooded and
fierce.

" The Divine Sappho did not think the island

THE CITY OF GOD

unworthy, as in her own sweet verses I will ask her
aid :

> and let thyself too
> Be my great ally.

"In the centre of Syracuse is a statue to the
splendour loving Pindar, and hear what he has
sung of that favoured land :

> The crests and clefts of the hills are asleep,
> And the headlands and ravines and foliage
> And all moving things that the dark earth nourishes,
> Wild hill haunting beasts, and the race of bees,
> And the creatures in the depths of the dark
> Glimmering ocean, and asleep are the tribes of
> The long winged birds.

"From that great singer I have learnt many
things of the doctrine of the Soul ; and of the
doctrine of numbers, which I am, as it were paid
to teach, most of my knowledge has come to me
from Sicily, where dwelt my Master, Pythagoras.

"So Syracuse in Scily has an attraction for me
greater than any other city, like a rope of many
different strands bound round about me it draws
me back.

"When my fate was spun by the Dread Ones a
thread was put in for Syracuse."

Simonides could no longer keep silent.

"I suppose its too much to ask anyone here to
say a good word for Athens. It used to be
considered equal to any city of the barbarians,
but we are become too big now, I suppose, to
worship the city where we were born."

THE CITY OF GOD

Plato paid no attention to his steward, but continued as if he was arguing with himself.

"I do not think we are at our best if we dwell in one city only. It is right enough that a man should love that place wherein his parents first brought him to the steps of the temple, and set his feet on the stairs that lead to heaven, but unless we have seen other cities, we cannot adequately love our own home.

"Another thing, our greatest poets have been the greatest travellers, making their hives not in one garden, but distilling their honey from the face of the whole earth. Note, too, that our greatest poems have been the stories of the great travellers and explorers, *The Wrath of Achilles*, *The Quest of Jason*, *The Wanderer*. The spirit of man struggling to free itself from the bonds of necessity is fast bound in Space and Time. We can struggle more effectively with Space than we can time Time, and all these are good and valid reasons for journeying often."

Neoptolemus interrupted him by saying: "Poor Athens! so soon to be widowed again, and that without even a semblance of regret."

Plato laughed: "You do not believe me, I see; but I can assure you I shall be very sorrowful to leave this dear city, but Athens is no longer the city of my dreams. When I was a young man I thought nothing could equal the glitter of this fair

THE CITY OF GOD

country, the keenness of the air and the alert observation of her citizens. The bright sunshine makes it a city for youth, but when you grow old you need a little shade to think in, and the firm heat of a Southern sun to warm your bones—either the darkness of the grave or the snow on a mountain lit by eternal fires.

" When I was young, I admit, I used to think that Sicily was a boorish country and Sparta a bovine community, but I know now that I need the restraint of Sparta and the warmth of Sicily, rather than the cold glitter of Athens."

" Glittering fiddlesticks," said Simonides, who never realised that Plato sometimes said these things not quite seriously.

" One thing I warrant ; you won't find a crowd of young men in this Sicily of yours fighting to pay fees to hear you talk."

" Perhaps not ", was the reply ; " but I shall see boys playing in the harbour sides, and hear boys laughing at their own jokes in the theatre ; it is better to hear them laughing at tyrants and poets than at the dull old men who can only give lectures."

" Well go to your Sicily," was all the slave could say, " but don't ask me to come."

Attis nodded his head : " That's what everyone says until they have lived in the island for a year. You pride yourself, Simonides, on your Attic

THE CITY OF GOD

culture, and you have never been as far from the city as a man's voice carries when he shouts. Yet you too would be happy in Sicily. But none of us can avoid what Fate has in store for us, and it was laid upon you, Plato, at birth to build new and perfect cities. You would be unworthy if you did not come over to Sicily to help us."

To my surprise Neoptolemus veered round : " That is quite true, Plato, you have explained so often, how Socrates undertook a journey over more treacherous and less charted seas that you have to compass, because duty called him, that you cannot well refuse, if indeed it is the true voice of Duty that you hear, and not merely an Echo from my neighbour here."

Simonides interrupted again : " What a fine herald you would make, talking of Death and Socrates. Don't talk to me about him.

" I remember him well enough, talking, talking, talking, all the night in this very room—a fat, little, ugly, devil, who went about asking questions, and now we must talk about him as if he were a God. He asked me his questions once, but I soon settled him."

" What did he ask you, O slave of my Master's friend ? ", said Attis.

" Oh, he only asked me one question ", said Simonides ; " I forget what it was, but I know I said : ' If you had so much to do as me, you

148

THE CITY OF GOD

would get on with your work, and not waste my time.'

" After that he left me alone.   If he came back to earth none of you would recognise him after talking him up the way you have.   I only hope when I'm dead and gone you'll say as pretty things of me.   But you won't, I'll be bound you'll be looking for as good a steward, and grumbling because you don't find him."

Neoptolemus answered him :   " That is very true.   I always say that when an old and valued servant dies, we shall never replace him—I say it with a sigh ; in fact, I remember saying exactly those words of three cooks, but somehow or other I always do replace them, Simonides, remember that, I always do."

I was not interested in hearing Simonides put in his place, but I was anxious to hear more about Socrates from those who knew him in the flesh, so hoping to inspire them, I said :   " Is it not always a fact that the characters of a writer, who knows his work, are more alive than the men of flesh and blood ? "   but it was Neoptolemus who felt it incumbent on him to speak for everyone :

" It is perfectly true, Euphorbion.   If anyone with literary ability should attempt to portray me, for example, in cold prose, no one would believe it.

" Readers would say that such perfection in mortal man could not be."

149

THE CITY OF GOD

Before anyone could reply to this astounding statement, he turned to Plato and continued :

" I knew Socrates, the real Socrates. Now your Socrates, the Socrates of your books, is a far fuller blooded individual, more virile and infinitely more amusing than our poor old friend.

" And, that being so, I will suggest something which will keep you fully occupied here in Athens instead of flitting away to this Sicily. Why don't you, with your gift for characterisation, and improvisation, and all the rest of it, or in other words making something out of nothing—re-write the lives of our Gods ? You should be able to make something of it if anybody could—their passions will be full blooded enough even for the Sicilian atmosphere although their intelligence is perhaps a little thin—like Sicilian wine.

" As you have been so convincing with Socrates, could you not write a realistic narrative concerning our deities ? You might even try and add a moral ? "

To all this my Master sat smiling.

" I remember ", he said, " saying something of the same sort to one who would have done the thing far better than I could. I begged Aristophanes to do this, and that led us on to talk of writing, and the labour of creative work in this sphere. Aristophanes asked me how I did my writing. But as you know that if you wish to learn, you

THE CITY OF GOD

must receive—you, Neoptolemus, will I know bear me out in this, so I asked him if he would tell me how he built his creations—and this is what Aristophanes said :

" ' I sit, and think, and somehow and sometime ideas come into my mind without sequence or plan, unasked and unquestioned. They come like babies, naked and unclothed—those were his very words—and when they arrived jumbled up, and like our own babies sometimes without a reputable father—first of all I fit them out with garments. These baby thoughts belong to anyone who will father them, but the clothes are out of my own individual store, and very much as the farmer registers his sheep with his own private mark—so these unfledged orphan thoughts become my property when I provide them with clothes. From this you will realise how much more Aristophanes would have been suited to write a realistic and convincing idyll of the Gods than I can ever be, for this is how I write.'

" My methods are much more practical, and dull, and prosaic. I sit down in my room, alone, with a virgin piece of paper before me, and as an idea comes, like a baby perhaps in that it has been conceived in the dark sometime before, but due none the less to emerge at the proper time—then I write it down. When in this way I have acquired a sufficient family, I reverse the processes of

151

THE CITY OF GOD

Nature, and proceed to marry my Muse, and set my progeny in due order.

"Then comes the real labour, if the metaphor will stand the strain, for each child of my Muse, has to be educated as it were into its position, and it becomes a question of geometry, that the greater should precede the lesser, or alphabetically that N should follow after M, in order that my Muse be not shamed; such, my friends, are the pains of my labour."

For the first time that evening the tutor of the Macedonians uncoiled himself from the silence, in which, like a crysallis he had been wound. "You are indeed fortunate, O Athenian. For my part I cannot find any relaxation in writing. The pains of labour I fully understand, but having, as it were, wrestled with boys, to make them express themselves in writing, I shun any similar wrestling with myself. To this extent only can I agree with what you have said, that the creations of the dramatist or the personages of the Dialogue are more vivid and real than the flesh and blood we meet in every day life.

"Take for example, the heroes of the old songs and fables, how alive and accurate and reasonable they are, they do all things well; yet, if we had met them in the flesh we should have deemed them either very simple or very incomprehensible, in fact very ordinary persons like ourselves.

152

THE CITY OF GOD

" This leads me on to something else said earlier in the evening to the effect that aliens are the best interpreters of poetry. Surely this is obvious, and it is inherently right that it should be so. So long as the poet confines himself to melody and a nice choice of words, there is no need for the interpreter, but should there be in the poetry a measure of inspiration in regard to ideas, it will only excite attention from his fellow citizens if the poet himself has gone outside the general ideas of the community in which he lives. So that the poet who achieves something in the realm of ideas will seem strange and foreign to his own city. These ideas will not be so strange to the alien, and I will go as far as to say that the more easily a poet can be understood by an alien, so much the more will his fellow citizens claim the poet as a genius. I should not put Homer in this particular temple, because his works are creative and artistic rather than inspirations."

No one seemed to wish to enter into these pedagogic depths, so that Attis answered, feeling that, after all, he was in part responsible for his own guest.

" But surely, Jason, after a harassing struggle with the minds of boys, it is a pleasant means of escape to create a dim world, shall we say, entirely free from children ? Although I cannot write myself, I love to retire in my mind to a country

THE CITY OF GOD

where there are no tyrants and no politics, and where the climate is as unlike Sicily as possible, and where there are no sea voyages, because there is no more sea. I picture this sanctuary to myself whenever I am at leisure, and more especially when I am tired, and from long habit I can reach this land of mine very swiftly. I return therefrom to the real earth much refreshed both in mind and body. Such pleasures as I enjoy in this way I had always imagined were a dim image of the joys of the dramatist who can pick and choose ideal companions, bone of his bone, and flesh of his flesh, with whom to pass his time."

These words excited my Master as much as a huntsman who has seen his hounds on their quarry. I knew the signs well enough, as he sat upright on his couch, with his hands clasped on the table before him lest they betray his emotions, and his eyes sparkling like a young boy's:

"Attis, my friend, you are mixing up two things —and you will forgive me if I speak with some measure of authority on these matters"—he turned to the rest of us—"Attis talked of the relaxing of the mind, and went on to insinuate that writing is first of all a relaxation (incidentally it is far too absorbing and laborious a habit of mind to be in any way a relaxation), and secondly that writing, or creating in writing, will lead the soul into the

THE CITY OF GOD

same country that the mind seeks in order to avoid the snares of the world.

" That may be so ; it depends on the disposition of the author, but the confusion in his mind lies in associating the creative powers of the mind with the creative powers of the Soul. Now the minds of most men can and do create a sort of refuge from the world, even if it only takes the form of speculating what we should do if we suddenly became very rich, or very famous, so too does the Soul speculate, but in a different direction.

" I will put it in another way, the creations of the mind may be people, or places or what you will, but they are always conditioned by place and time, the desires of the Soul are free from these trammels.

" I will give you an example to explain what I mean.

" Let us take Aristophanes, his name among many others because his name has already been mentioned.

" His body lived in Athens, but his plays, the creations of his mind, came from a country in some respects very like Attica but habited in general by a more delightful people. The Soul of Aristophanes struggling with his doubts and fears left a magic touch on the creations of his mind (for what is genius but this) but could not find a resting place

THE CITY OF GOD

even in Cloud-Cuckoo-Land. I say this because Aristophanes was an unhappy man, his bitterness was the result of his mind not being able to share with his Soul the treasures of heaven.

"Each one of us, whether writer or not, has need of two havens, or heavens, where the mind and Soul can find rest, and if these two havens can be found together, happiness or contentment will follow.

"I am fortunate because my mind and my Soul in their search have found a country where they can be content together."

Neoptolemus broke in : "I know what you are going to say, Plato—Dreams, the land of the sleep-walkers."

"Your courtesy has misled you ", said my Master. "No my friend, the land of dreams is not always a pleasant land. Let me illustrate this by the words of Odysseus :

"'If I climb up the slope of the shady wood and lie down to rest in the thick bushwood, in the hope that the cold and weariness might leave me, and if sweet sleep comes over me, I fear me lest I become a prey and spoil to wild beasts.'

"How right is Homer in this ! The country of our dreams is too often overrun with wild beasts who will not be tamed, and are by no means pleasant companions."

"Well then ", said Neoptolemus, in no way

THE CITY OF GOD

abashed and determined to have his say, "this country of oblivion and happiness combined can be found together in the arms of a lover."

But Attis answered him: "O Athenian, I can answer you, for I am older than Plato and I have seen more cities than any of you, since my fate has sent me to and fro like a shuttle over sea and land. I have sought all my days for this dear land, and never refrained from asking anyone whom I thought would prove a guide to lead me where I fain would be. I have spoken hopefully to many maidens who bear pitchers of wine, in the hope that they may be the Goddess. But these maidens invariably lead us to a country from which we must needs return to earth disappointed, either with a bitter taste or a sad memory, so that we are driven to search afresh more vehemently than ever for a refuge, for the country of our hopes. I thought once as you do now, perhaps it is my misfortune not to have found this refuge on the earth."

The gaunt stranger followed the sense of the argument, and he muttered to himself and shook his head, and Jason continued to appear interested and disapproving at the same time, so, that there I alone remained to find a good word for love.

It did not become me, I thought, to speak my thoughts out loud, but I did not intend to forego my intentions whatever a stranger or even an Athenian might say.

157

THE CITY OF GOD

My Master with his unerring perception and tact saw what was uppermost in my mind, and relieved me from speaking :

" It would be unnatural for you, Euphorbion, at your age to pay attention to Attis, or even me, in this matter. Do not despair, but rather remember that love is a climate rather than a country, and that love must be shared to be enjoyed. I do not think that you will find it entirely restful. Whereas what we are discussing is a country (which has no existence) and can only be enjoyed alone and moreover is entirely foreign to the thoughts of youth, since it is the creation of our old age, and becomes of increasing importance the older we get. Which of us here present has not followed after this will-o'-the-wisp we call love, in the hope that we should find a state of being where we should be safe from the troubles of our ordinary life."

Neoptolemus interrupted him : " I will admit that I have embraced every opportunity that came my way, but my motives were much simpler than yours, Plato."

" You have been perhaps too rich, Neoptolemus, to feel the troubles of the ordinary man, and you have been far too comfortable to desire anything but your usual life. Love with you is as much an appetite as anything else, a craving of the body. This craving for another state of being has its

158

THE CITY OF GOD

mental side as well as its physical side, and if I am right in my surmise the Soul also has similar desires. For that reason I say that this desire for another country where the mind may be fully at rest is not an affair of youth, because the quest of love is quite sufficiently engrossing during the first years of our manhood, when however the hunting becomes wearisome, or the body fails, the mind takes charge and drives abroad seeking that happiness which the body by itself is unable to supply.

"So much for the desires of the body. The mind then begins to assert itself, demanding in its turn some fulfilment. In my case my mind has an Odyssey of its own still incomplete. Even before my body had finished with love, I hankered after politics, I believe that many other young men are afflicted in the same way, and I was offered a position in the Government, but the death of Socrates, my Master and my greatest friend, estranged me, both from my political acquaintances and my aspirations for office.

"At a certain age one is inclined to take oneself seriously, and, being infected with this disease at the time, I decided to seek wisdom, but like many other searchers after truth, I made a false start.

"I remember thinking that the peace of mind I desired was to be found in the accumulation of knowledge. I soon found out that the mere

THE CITY OF GOD

adding to what I knew, or understood, was but an additional burden to carry.

"The next step led me to believe that there existed a secret wisdom which would bring balm to my mind, so that I wasted many years looking for it everywhere but in the right place. I went hot foot to the philosophers, but at that age it seemed impossible that what was published so openly could contain a secret wisdom, and those of you who have been in the same position will know that the desire for exclusive possession is common both to the lover and those who hunger after the mysteries. I could not feel that what had been handled by so many in the market place could be balm for my Soul, which wanted something for itself.

"Still hopeful I essayed the Mysteries themselves. The guardians of the secrets were discouraging— I have since learnt that they make it a rule of set purpose to discourage both the novice and the enthusiast, lest the Holy Places be profaned by the unworthy—nevertheless, I waited at Eleusis, almost burnt up with the hopes that the name of the place inspired."

Jason interrupted him : " How far were you initiate ? ", he asked. " The Degree of Apollo ", said my Master. " And you ", continued Jason, turning to Attis, who made a sign with his hands that I could not see, and replied, in these words :

160

THE CITY OF GOD

" Well found and all seeing, O builder of Temples."
To which the Macedonian replied : " The hope of
the Corner Stone."

He then turned to my Master : " You said just
now that the guardians of our Mysteries seemed
to discourage you. That is perfectly true, for many
come like you hoping for a knowledge that will
completely satisfy them, and in some fashion make
them immune from all evil in the future without
any effort on their own part ; such as these are
not worthy of the Food of the Gods, and rightly
I think do we discourage mere idle curiosity.

" Attis and I have progressed more on this
Way, and Hamilcar I believe is of the Magi, so he
can confirm what I say." The stranger nodded
and opened his tunic and made bare to them what
seemed to me a small red stone he wore round his
neck.

" It is difficult to speak before strangers ",
continued Jason, " lest what should be hidden is
betrayed ; but I can say this openly—There is
no such thing as a secret knowledge or formula
which can protect the Soul, or satisfy the mind.
Neither the Mysteries of Eleusis or of Orpheus
provide an incantation to open the door of
knowledge of Good and Evil, though there be many
who believe that they do.

" The Soul cannot be protected by anything
external to herself, nor can the mind be sated with

THE CITY OF GOD

the knowledge that we impart. It is true that you will learn a great deal by seeking admission to the mysteries, but the search will not be rewarded in the way that you expect. I will admit that initiation, which is accompanied by a restraint of the human passions and appetites, has a beneficial effect, but any effort of restraint is generally an advantage "—and with these words Jason looked at Neoptolemus with contempt, but without any success as the fat Athenian continued to eat grapes with the air of an adept. " All that man in general can learn from the earlier degrees of the Mysteries is a perception of the working of the heart, he will not snatch, as so many hope, a series of passwords which can open the gates of eternal life. If I could make epigrams, I would say that many may be called, but few are chosen, the successful adepts are those who renounce rather than those who grasp."

" I would agree with you, Plato ", he continued : " I question very much if knowledge by itself can satisfy the mind or the Soul. I could speak feelingly on this matter, because I have spent so much of my time trying to impart knowledge—of sorts—to the immature, and as I grow older it becomes increasingly pathetic to find out how vainly parents hope for great things for their children in as much as they give them the means to acquire knowledge.

THE CITY OF GOD

" Fortunately the Gods have arranged that the Soul of a child does not suffer any permanent harm in the process of education, in as much as the Soul is secure enough in its habitation to resist succesfully the onslaught of anything physical.

" I am not so certain that the minds of children escape harm in the process. Therefore I say it is unreasonable to seek in knowledge, however occult or free from taints of universality, any real freedon or refuge."

As he finished speaking Hamilcar raised his head and spoke as follows :

" You say refuge, Jason. The search for occult knowledge is not without risk to body, mind and spirit. The risk is that the search for such knowledge, whether it exists or not, is attended with greater dangers than you have mentioned. I will tell you a story which will bear me out.

" Setna the Son of Ramaases, king of Egypt, thirsted for this knowledge of which you speak, so much so that he went down alive into the world of the Departed and forcibly laid hands on the Book of Magic, which contained the words that he fain would know. Neither the dead king, nor Akura his wife, nor even the tiny body of Merab, their little son, who were the guardians of that Book, could deter him from the theft which he had in his mind. And having stolen the book, and having acquired a knowledge, which he could

163

THE CITY OF GOD

not control, it was only by the sacrifice of his life, his wife, and all that he deemed sacred that he could recover his sanity. Beware then, my friends, of seeking this knowledge, unless you are shielded either by a pure heart or at least some training in these matters."

"Our host to-night", said Attis, as the stranger ceased, "has some verses of his own which are applicable :

> Mariners may be safe on sea and land,
> But know that this tomb ye are passing
> Is that of a shipwrecked man, who lost his bearings.

This search for hidden knowledge is dangerous and leads to death."

My Master at these words got up from his couch and continued speaking walking up and down the room.

"This is all very terrifying, but I have long ago come to the conclusion that this secret knowledge of yours could not comfort me. Somehow or other, I learnt that my hunger or thirst, was not of the mind but the Soul, and these desires of the Soul must be satisfied or the Soul will die, very much as our bodies die if we only keep from food and drink long enough. Now to most of us, unless we travel, or shall I say, receive fresh mental food— I will except you, Neoptolemus—become old mentally, and die. In the same way the Soul desires to travel in her own fashion, more especially

164

THE CITY OF GOD

perhaps when the body and the mind are weary, more still when the body is in pain—and as the mind can build a haven wherein the body is soothed and lulled to rest—incarnate and created by herself, so too the Soul must create for itself a refuge which is none the less real because it cannot be seen. It is of this country that I have been speaking."

As he passed me, my love for him overcame me and I plucked his robe as he passed, for I knew what was passing in his mind. " Master ", I said, " is it not possible after all for both these places to be the same ? "

" Yes ", he said, " but you have my secret."

They all looked at me, but I could not reply until my Master, continuing his walk, said : " You tell them ; some of them will understand."

" I can guess ", said Neoptolemus—" it's Sicily."

" No, you are wrong ", I said ; " but Sicily is on the way."

" How can that be ", said Attis—" have we not agreed the place we are thinking about has no existence in time or space. It has to be—and he held up his hands and counted on his fingers— first a climate where the body may be soothed, secondly an atmosphere where the mind is at peace, thirdly the soul is to be supreme therein and free to travel without let or hindrance. It sounds like

165

THE CITY OF GOD

a Platonic Olympus. That is not true of Sicily. None the less, you say, Sicily is on the way."

"Let me help you", said the Macedonian. "Remember that the imagination of man has always turned to golden lands towards the West, therefore it is to the setting sun that we must turn. Sicily is in this direction, and is therefore 'on the way'.

"That voyage, too, has a spice of danger, like your secret knowledge, for many have sought the land of the Hesperides, and no message has come back from those travellers.

"The bodies, together with the minds of these voyagers, have been given to the wine dark sea. May be the setting sun has consumed their ashes."

"Or the fires of Poseidon", said Attis. "I cannot help thinking that Sicily, Plato, is in some way connected with the country that you are seeking. Is not that island the land of Poseidon —it is a cruel land, I will admit, but Poseidon is masterful and cruel in his own element, as you have said. I will confess I am afraid when I see the white waves of the horsemen who follow his chariot on the high seas. Plato tell me! Is it that this land of yours is not land at all, but a vast ocean.

"Over the ocean the will of the Gods is Law, the waves are raised and stilled by the working of the mind of their Creator, over this expanse your mind may cruise and fly to and fro, like a seagull,

THE CITY OF GOD

gently and happily in spirit form in an eternal and soft evening breeze."

"No, no!", said my Master, laughing and very happy—"my land is indeed land, and not sea; and furthermore I believe it exists. It is the land of both Poseidon and Athens—and you and I will share its joys because you and I are the descendants of the citizens of this dear country of mine. Sweet are the voices in that land, and sweet the fruit that grows therein, and such is the country which the poet has described as the Garden of Alcinous in those verses which Euphorbion recited earlier in this evening. I have never been to this land, but I believe in its actual existence both in Time and Space."

As my Master spoke, one by one the lamps went out, as if in receipt of some hidden message, and one only remained alight, and that was the one over my Master's couch. In the gloom, without apparently noticing anything, he continued in a voice growing warmer as his interest outgrew his natural diffidence in disclosing his innermost thoughts. "Time and Space! I confess I am not sure, if either of these things really exist, but when I say this City of mine exists both in Time and Space I mean that it really was, and is, as much a city, and with as decided life of its own, as Athens has to-day.

" After all Time is but a girdle for the Olympians,

167

THE CITY OF GOD

which can contain, but is unable to retain the Eternal Verities ! and Space is only another name for Everywhere "—and smiling round the table, he went on : " you will admit you can always put Anything in Everywhere."

" I said I have never visited this island continent, but my mind is constantly—there he paused before saying—in Atlantis, for such is the name of this place. I have come to believe that Atlantis, the great city of my island is indeed that City of God, wherein both my mind and my Soul shall find their rest and comfort. I firmly believe that my body too would be equally at home therein, if only it could survive the journey and reach the haven of its hopes.

" This City of God has in some fashion been present with me since I was born, or rather since I could remember. Perhaps I alone of my generation have spent a previous existence within its walls, or, and I think this is more probable, I have been permitted to retain these visions, in which I rejoice, and hoard up like a miser.

" All men, I believe, have some recollection of their former lives, but with the majority the cares of this present world, or their companions, or misfortune, blurr the slender vision of their eternity, at any rate, I have never yet met anyone who as much as recognises this home of mine.

" I have a quarrel with the hymn-writers over

THE CITY OF GOD

this, for the City of God is often referred to in those poems we learn as children, but for some reason or other the composers make it of so material a character that no child can think of this land but as an eternal chorus of a musical nature or a sort of perpetual feast.

" As we get older we are still hampered with these inflictions of our childhood, that are so utterly unlike the visions that our souls have been permitted to enshrine.

" These writers should remember the words of one of their own number :

" ' Narrow is the path, merciless the necessity, but broad is the road for him who speaks amiss.'

" But to return to this great and dear country of mine, when, like an exile, I feel compelled by the love I bear for my lost home to talk thereon, no one will believe that I am speaking the truth—some even, have been unkind enough to suggest that the history of my spiritual home, that I have been called upon to describe, was but the achievement of my imagination. None of you, for you know me too well, would waste your time or mine, casting aspersions on the veracity of my description of Atlantis (because you have not read it perhaps), still less would you read what I have written if you thought that I could attempt to deceive.

" None the less within this City of mine, the

169

THE CITY OF GOD

word of God is supreme, of Laws there are none, because the will of the Good is sufficient.

" Therein is no evil present because when God is supreme only good can exist, no evil person can breathe that rarified air.

" So much so that I fear that the passengers thereto, of which my mind would be one, will be compelled to leave behind them, as they go, an increasing part of themselves the nearer they get.

" Peaceful in the midst of trouble, and free from all spirit of envy and enmity, therein is no darkness in the Country of my Dreams. Everywhere is a light, bland and serene, and it is obvious that the nearer we get to the West so much the less is the journey of the Chariot of the Sun ; of that land it is true ' There is no darkness with Thee, for darkness and light are both alike.'

" I hope to find within that island continent the shades of my friends who have departed this life to struggle with the immensity of cloud that lay about their departing, in no way have they lost final touch with the friends they have left behind. Socrates assuredly will be there, still asking questions, Simonides, and still receiving answers that have no direct relation to the question.

" Aristophanes will be there, though I can well believe that some of the inhabiters will already have quarrelled with him ; but it will be of no

THE CITY OF GOD

avail, for his seat among the Immortals will be firm enough to defy even his own logic. There some happy day, will my soul also be, like an infant lisping my guesses at truth and whatever else evades me "—and here Plato almost laughed out loud—" because truth is like Nausicaa, more interested in cleaning old garments than in mere questions of prudery.

" There, too, will the Poet triumph, not without rivals perhaps, but, drinking a nectar that we cannot brew here below, will be inspired with Poetry what is greater than immortality, and beyond even the inspiration of Hermes, the Heavenly Messenger.

" Such ideas as have come to my mental mind, I feel convinced are babies born in that more favourable clime and are translated from their heavenly womb through my poor brain—I will go further, the aspirations of our greatest minds are but the reflections of a childhood spent in a heavenly atmosphere.

" The flowers and the fruit of the spirit of man are born there, and we can but perceive them— here he paused for an instant—as reflections in a mirror.

" Therefore, with high hopes, shall I leave this City for Sicily ; not without many and deep regrets, but with sure and certain knowledge that I am taking one stride towards a home that has

THE CITY OF GOD

been built for me elsewhere, and as I step into this boat, that Attis has prepared for my voyage, I shall say this prayer to Poseidon—or Zeus :

" ' O my Father, which art in Heaven—Do thou now make ready for me a vessel, high and stout, such as Dymas himself could build. Therein will I place, neither raiment nor gear nor gold, but only such food as will last for a short journey, for I would fain be with Thee.'

" Having said this prayer, I will set forth on the sea, doubting nothing. I will choose only a night when the evening breeze setting softly from the land leads dulcet (that is a poetic word, I think) towards the setting sun. I am assured that I shall, either this night that Attis chooses, or some other, inevitably find myself in this land that I was born to seek—though when I reach it I am certain it will look different from what I have imagined—this City of God. But, however or wherever it may be, nevertheless this will still be true of my City," and our conversation finished that night with Plato reciting these words :

" Neither is it shaken by winds, nor ever wet with rain, nor does snow fall uopn it, but the air is outspread, clear and cloudless, and over it hovers a radiant whiteness.

" Therein the blessed Gods are glad all their days."